A Guide for
Child-Care
Workers

MORRIS FRITZ MAYER Ph.D.

THE CHILD WELFARE LEAGUE OF AMERICA

67 IRVING PLACE • NEW YORK, NEW YORK 10003

Child Welfare League of America
440 First Street, NW, Suite 310, Washington, DC 20001-2085

Current printing (last number)

20   19   18   17   16   15   14   13   12   11   10

Printed in the United States of America
Library of Congress Catalog Card Number: 58-10171
ISBN # 0-87868-0667

Contents

3 MEALS AND THE MEANING OF FOOD 57

4 THE DAY HAS TWENTY-FOUR HOURS 77

Foreword

Changing concepts in the field of institutional care for children are currently reflected in the programs of many institutions throughout the country. The child welfare field has been witnessing the continuous transformation of children's institutions in keeping with current knowledge of children's needs. Devotion of considerable thought to program content within the institutional setting has brought about a deeper, more realistic understanding of the most effective utilization of all institutional staff.

We know now that every person who comes in contact with a child who must live away from his parents has a meaning for the child, whether it be positive or negative. This is as true for the child who is living in an institution for emotionally disturbed children as for the child who is hospitalized or who must live in any other type of group setting.

While much has been written about the role of the caseworker and other professional staff, the significance of the child-care staff has been dealt with less extensively. In undertaking to publish this book, the League hopes that those both in and outside the institutional setting will welcome this organized presentation of knowledge and practice governing the role of the child-care staff.

The Child Welfare League is pleased that Dr. Morris Fritz Mayer was able to undertake this timely assignment. Because of his depth of understanding and broad scope of experience, particularly in the institutional field, it seems most appropriate that Dr. Mayer should present this aspect of the intricate operation of institutional care.

In assembling this material, the author offers to all those who are closely involved with the care of the child recognition of the importance of their respective roles; and to the child himself, reassurance of our continued responsibility to make sure that he is provided with the service and care that he needs.

JOSEPH H. REID
Executive Director,
Child Welfare League of America

Preface

Every experienced institutional worker knows that the people in charge of the children's daily lives, who live with them in their cottages, dormitories, or wards, and supervise their daily activities, are the closest approximation to a "parent" figure an institution can provide. Their functions at the institution resemble in many ways the functions of the parent in the family. In some institutions their official title, "houseparent" or "cottage parent," indicates their parental function. Their importance and the need to provide them with the working conditions, training and professional status essential to their role has been stressed throughout the literature on institutional care. Leading social workers, such as Eva Burmeister, Gisela Konopka, Alan-Keith-Lucas, and above all, Susanne Schulze, have been the champions of this group of workers and have pioneered in the establishment of city and state-wide in-service training programs. Welfare federations and state departments of welfare have allocated funds for this purpose, and in recent years some universities have included courses for houseparents in their program.

Most professional writing in this specific field is *about* "houseparents" rather than for them. It is directed mainly to institutional administrators and social workers in order to help them give the proper emphasis to this category of workers in the organization, integration and budget of the institution.

This book is written for those who give day-to-day care to children in an institution, no matter what its purpose—that is, childcare workers in institutions for dependent children, for the emotionally disturbed, for the delinquent or retarded in training schools, or for sick children in mental hospitals. I have deliberately abstained from calling them houseparents, since this title is a misnomer. There are two main reasons why the title of child-care worker should not include the concept of parent substitute. (1) Since in modern institutions most children have at least one living parent, nothing should permit the misinterpretation that institutional care is meant to be substitute family care and that "houseparents" are substitute parents. Children who come to an institution these days can, we hope, return to their families after a relatively short stay; and if there is no own family available for them, they can, we hope, be placed with substitute parents in a real family.

(2) One of the major advantages of institutional treatment is the availability of many potential parent figures from whom the child can choose the one he wants to invest with parental identification. This may be the caseworker or the cook, the psychiatrist or the gardener, the teacher or the administrator. It may well be the child-care worker and in a majority of cases it is. This identification with a parent figure depends on the child's readiness for such a relationship, and is largely determined by his past experiences with his own parents. It is always the child who decides this. Any administrative assignment to "parenthood"—even in title only— seems to me harmful rather than helpful to the child at the institution.

I have chosen, therefore, the title of child-care worker for this discussion. I refer to child-care workers in the masculine gender although more of them are women, and there are some particularly feminine functions which call for the services of a woman. In some of these places I have used the feminine gender. This is marked by a footnote.

While this book is written mainly for child-care workers, it should be of interest to workers of other disciplines who deal with children at institutions. Certainly professionals of all disciplines have contributed to the thoughts expressed here. I am particularly indebted to all my colleagues at Bellefaire for their assistance in the formulation of these concepts.

Most of all I have learned from the child-care workers, at Bellefaire and in many other organizations, with whom over the years I have discussed most of the ideas presented here. It is impossible to list all the sources and people who have helped me prepare this book. A summary "thank you" is all that can be offered here. Two names, however, must be mentioned. Special thanks go to Mrs. Henrietta L. Gordon and the staff of the Child Welfare League of America for the many suggestions on the content and the careful editing of the manuscript; and to my secretary, Mrs. Gussie Cohen, for her indefatigable and always cheerful help.

This book is offered as a guide rather than an outline of duties. Such an outline or manual would have to be written by individual institutions in accordance with their specific situations. The first few chapters discuss the individual child and his interaction with the group. In Chapter Four (The Day Has Twenty-four Hours) the routines of daily living are examined. The complex and often controversial subjects of play and discipline are explored in the next two chapters. The problems of cooperation and communication with other members of the staff are discussed in the chapter on teamwork. The final chapter considers the training of child-care workers.

The aim of this book is to help people think about their jobs and find their own answers, rather than to give these answers. It is, so to speak, an appetizer for child-care workers, rather than the main dish. I hope it will stimulate their curiosity to explore the subject further and increase their love for the important work they do.

Introduction

The Role of the Child-Care Worker at the Institution

Everyone who works in a children's institution is an "educator" of the children. A little girl of seven who runs to the switchboard operator's cove in the hall of the office building, and is overwhelmed by all the flickering lights, wires, contacts, and plugs, wants to know what this is all about, how it operates. Of course, she must be prevented from pulling out the connections, but the switchboard operator who in a not too busy moment explains to her all the confusing and amazing things helps in her education—and in this sense is her teacher.

> Then there is Johnny, who is fourteen years old. He came to the institution because at thirteen years of age he stole a car. Johnny is fascinated by cars, and by anything mechanical. He discovers the new snow-plow near the garage of the institution. He just can't move on to the chores that he is supposed to do. He must find out about this new machine. He goes to Mr. O'Brien who operates the plow. He asks how many horsepower it has, what kind of engine, how much snow it can shovel at one time. He sure would like to drive that new gadget himself.

Mr. O'Brien explains to him how it operates, then sends him kindly off to his chores. Besides being a good mechanic, Mr. O'Brien has become an educator.

Sometimes this education is a little difficult. Billy, for instance, is a mischievous little ten-year-old, an angry boy who feels that the whole world is against him. He has just walked through the mud, and comes back to the cottage as the maid is about to wash the floors. He insists on walking over the floor with his muddy shoes, and the maid insists he clean his shoes first, or change them. Billy refuses to do so. The maid shows him how to get to the shoe closet without walking through the living room. Billy becomes very angry, but the maid insists firmly and kindly that he abide by the rules of orderly living. Billy does not like this, but finally he gives in. The maid has become an educator.

The maid, the mechanic, and the switchboard operator were not hired to be educators, but at the institution they are. In addition to these unplanned-for "educators" there are the trained educators —or in a wider sense all those whose major job is care of the children—teachers, tutors, recreational workers, caseworkers, group workers, psychologists, psychiatrists, nurses, doctors, chaplains, administrators. Their work is geared toward improving the child's physical, intellectual, emotional and social development. For years prior to their coming to the institution they have prepared themselves for this work. They are experts in one special category of human relationships.

And then there are the child-care workers. To them this book is dedicated. They are known in different institutions under different names, such as cottage parents, houseparents, supervisors, social teachers, counselors. Their education and background, their hours of work and their pay differ as widely as their titles, but all of them are educators. They supervise the children in everyday life from the time they get up in the morning to the time they go to bed, and through the night if necessary. They are not trained educators nor specialists in any field of the science of man. Yet, at the institution they are the chief educators of all. They are not teachers of arithmetic nor Spanish, mental hygiene nor basketball. They teach the child how to live. They are not experts in any specific field. They help the child in all fields of living—how to sit at a table, how to dress, how to clean up a room, how to take medicine, how to get along with the other children, how to write a letter home and, yes, how to do his arithmetic homework. They are the experts in the art of living.

Their job is especially difficult when the child does not want to learn these things . . . and many children in the institution do not. Teachers' methods of instruction differ, but all have one thing in common—the aim that the child should enjoy learning

Similarly the teaching of the art of everyday living has the goal that living can be fun. The child-care worker not only tries to teach the child the skills of mastering the demands of everyday living in our society, but also the ability to find enjoyment in this social living.

The child-care worker is not the expert or specialist, but the universal educator of the child at the institution. The success of all other educators depends on his ability to help the child use their education and their skills. The child-care worker may not be able to resort to a store of accumulated learning, but in order to be successful, he has to give of himself. He need not be able to compete with the knowledge of the experts, but he has to match them in wisdom day in and day out.

CHAPTER 1

The Child as an Individual

Who are the children at the institution? Are they like other children? Does their coming to an institution mean that they are different? Does the stay at the institution accentuate this difference? These are a few of the questions often raised about children in an institution. Some people tend to answer these questions by denying any difference and maintaining that these children are "just like any other children." Other people emphasize the difference so much that children in institutions, especially emotionally disturbed and delinquent youngsters, seem almost to be a separate species of the human race.

Above all, children in institutions are children. Their basic characteristics and needs are the same as those of any other children. Their similarity to the rest of the child population far outweighs any differences. In order to understand institutional children one has to understand children. However, differences do exist in their development, and these differences quite often are the main reasons for their coming to the institution. There are differences in their life experiences, due to their separation from their parents; and there are differences in their living experiences, if only the fact that they live in groups. We will now look at individual children and see the main factors determining their development and growth.

Needs of the Child

While every child is an individual, there are many characteristics and needs common to all children. All children have certain basic needs which must be met, if their physical, emotional, social and intellectual development is to be healthy. If these needs are not met the lack may show itself in many harmful ways.

From birth on all children need proper nutrition, proper clothing, health care, protection from outside dangers and from their own impulses. Parents are the major protectors of children. In cases where parents are unable to protect the children from dangers around them and within them, the children lose confidence in their parents and become frightened. Sometimes they act out this fright in a bravado manner by disregarding dangers, and sometimes by exaggerating their fears and thinking that there is a danger lurking in every corner.

Children must feel wanted. They must be convinced that their parents love them and do not just tolerate them; that society has a use for them; that their families look forward to being with them; and that they bring satisfaction and joy to people by their mere existence. Unfortunately, many children do not have this assurance. Social, economic, and physical pressures on their parents interfere with joyful acceptance of their children, and the children become morose, insecure, and bitter. This deprivation affects their whole lives, unless they receive help. The child who receives love and joyful acceptance will carry the benefits of such an acceptance throughout his life, in school, in his work, and later on in his own family. He feels that he can contribute something in his own way to his society and that by his very existence he enriches the social group in which he lives.

Every child needs to be directed. As he grows older, the child must know that he can trust the people who are responsible for him, that they can teach him what is right and wrong, good and bad. The child must see that his parents have educational, social, and moral standards which they are eager to attain, and for which they are ready to make sacrifices. Accepting these values is sometimes hard for the child. He might resist some of them, yet he wants and needs them. As the child sees from early life on that his parents subject themselves to a value system, he accepts values himself, and can slowly build up a conscience of his own. Parents who become upset if their child cheats in school but are themselves engaged in shady business; parents who would not tolerate their child's using vile language, but engage in fighting with each other or in alcoholic excess, cannot really direct the child to a value system.

Increasingly as a child grows older he has to feel that his parents trust him; that they have confidence in his inherent goodness, and that they want him to become an independent person. If parents overwhelm a child with suspicion, reproaches, and unnecessary limitations, they handicap his development. If they can accept him, especially in adolescence, even if he deviates momentarily from the parental pattern and value system, he may well develop a value system of his own. Basic trust has to be built up in children very early. Children who come to the institution often have the feeling of not being trusted and trustworthy. Indeed they have often committed acts which strained people's trust in them beyond the breaking point. Institutional workers have a doubly hard job then—to protect these children and to re-establish their feelings of being trusted.

While these four basic needs are to be met in all children, the child in the institution has a particular need to have them satisfied. At the same time many social and psychological hurdles block the fulfillment of these needs. The child-care worker, whose function is to teach the child how to live and how to find fun in life, has a particularly difficult task.

Reasons for Coming to the Institution

Teaching children how to live socially and enjoy it is not easy under any circumstances. Teaching it to children in institutions is a complicated and difficult assignment. Children who are away from their own homes have usually gone through very painful experiences. Some have had to leave because their homes were broken up, some because of some special handicap which could be dealt with only in an institution; others because their behavior made removal necessary. Many have more reason to hate life than to like it; to defy and ignore society's standards than to submit to them. They often resist being taught these standards. They often resent the people who want to teach them. If you would tell them that it is "fun" to live by social rules, they would not understand, or they would laugh bitterly.

Let us look at them a little closer.

Years ago, when death, sickness or divorce interrupted the normal course of family life, children were often sent to an institution to stay for many years. Today, through such services as Aid to Dependent Children and family and children's services, we try to keep the family intact. The majority of children from broken homes, therefore, stay in their own home.

We have learned during the past fifty years that there is no substitute for an own family, and that even a second-rate own family is better than a first-rate substitute. We have also learned that living in a family is a most important need for any child, even the one who cannot live in his own. Therefore, a large number of children from broken homes who cannot live in their own families live in substitute families, such as foster homes, boarding homes, or relative's homes.

Relatively few children are sent to institutions only because their homes are broken. There must be other reasons why children whose only problem is that their families broke up, cannot live with a foster family. Sometimes the reason has to do with the parents. While they cannot keep the child at home, they do not permit him to live in another family. They resent the foster parents, are jealous of foster mothers, and fearful of losing their children to these "other" parents. Until they have been helped to change their attitudes it is often inadvisable to use a foster home for their child. Such a placement would bring the child into serious confusion, and might make his adjustment in the foster home impossible. These parents may need time and more casework help before they can cooperate with a foster home.

Sometimes the reason a child cannot live with a foster family lies within the child. This is the case in children of newly divorced parents who have not yet adjusted to their new uprootedness, and cannot accept living in "another" family. It might be the case in homes that broke up rather suddenly because of illness, death, or sudden catastrophes, that children cannot adjust to the intimate and personal atmosphere of a substitute family and need time in a more neutral and less personal environment, such as the institution offers.

Quite often the reason a child of a broken home cannot go into a foster home arises from a community situation—the shortage of adequate foster homes, often due to the lack of trained social workers to work with foster parents, or the inadequate remuneration of foster parents. In some instances community prejudices against foster homes prevent children from receiving the care considered most appropriate to their needs.

Children with special handicaps such as deafness, blindness, mental defectiveness, or severe neurological or other organic disorders must often be cared for in institutions because the medical, educational and vocational facilities cannot be provided on the outside. Fortunately our society is in the process of providing more and more facilities to keep as many of these children as possible in their own communities. Thus classes for the mentally retarded, for the hard of hearing, for certain types of brain injured children, and for sight saving, are being established, in many communities, as part of the school system or supplementary to it. Much more needs to be done to prevent children from having to be removed from their homes. Where the line between home care and institutional care for these children will ultimately be drawn is hard to say. At present many physically handicapped children are in institutions. The purpose of institutionalization is mainly education—training to enable those for whom it is possible to lead relatively normal lives in the community. This goal may not be achieved for the more seriously handicapped ones, but an ever-increasing number of these children can return to their homes. While they are in the institution, these children need special care in relation to their special handicaps. However, above all they need to learn how to live, how to become social human beings, and how to find pleasure in life. The ultimate aim of the institutional child-care worker, therefore, is mainly the same as that of any other person caring for children. In the past few decades, the increasing number of children with behavior problems has been of great concern to our society. Schools, social agencies, juvenile courts, and, above all, parents themselves have been distressed about an apparently ever-growing number of these children. Some of these problems express themselves in the child's withdrawal, depression, and timidity. Others show themselves in aggressiveness, destructiveness, defiance of adult authority and of the social order. Often both types of problems are accompanied by physical symptoms, such as nervous tics, bedwetting, nail biting, sleeplessness, or stomach disorders. Fortunately, parents themselves quite often are concerned about the problems early enough to ask for help from a psychiatrist, a child guidance clinic, or a family agency before the problem gets out of hand. In such cases the child can remain in his own home and receive help there. In many cases, however, the behavior disorder is already of such proportions that help in the own home cannot be given and the child has to be placed.

Not infrequently the courts order the removal of these children from home because of delinquent behavior. These are the children committed to training schools. Others of this group are in special residential centers where they receive treatment. A great number of them are in institutions that do not have special treatment facilities, as county homes or dependency institutions. They present a major problem of management and education. They are the "children who hate" everybody, most of all themselves. They are the most serious problems for child-care workers. Yet, no matter how their behavior manifests itself, whether they come voluntarily or by court commitment, whatever the specific treatment plan for these children is—above all they are children, young, confused human beings who have lost faith in themselves and in their world.

We know today that all behavior has causes, that it is not just an arbitrary, willful expression but has its origin in past experiences and present unfulfilled needs. It takes a long time and special skill to find what these causes are. They are unknown not only to the adult dealing with the child, but also to the child himself. Only as one discovers these causes can one help the child. Almost always some of the causes lie in the relationship between the child and his parents, and in an inner and often unconscious anger the child feels toward them. He often transfers this anger to other people who represent parent figures to him. Child-care workers are, therefore, frequently the innocent targets of the child's unconscious anger against his own parents.

The Separation Experience

While the emotionally disturbed child has deeper and longer-lasting behavior disorders, every child who is taken away from his own home has either overt or covert temporary emotional disturbances. A child's separation from his parents leaves him feeling abandoned. He asks himself whether he is worthwhile. He wonders what is wrong with him. He feels inferior, rejected, lonely. He wonders why this had to happen to him and not to other children, perhaps not even to his own brothers and sisters. He thinks he might have done something which has caused the family breakdown. A handicapped child may think that some wrongdoing on his part might have caused not only his separation from his parents, but also his handicap. There is no logic in this, but emotions do not submit themselves to the laws of logic. Thus, all children in institutions have some emotional problems, if only temporary ones caused by the separation experience.

As far as the child-care worker's role with the children is concerned, the difference in handling the various kinds of children in an institution is more of degree than of kind. The suggestions made here, therefore, ought to apply, with certain variations, to all children in all institutions.

Age Differences

In a little handbook like this, one cannot give a detailed description of the differences in developmental stages of children. As we describe the role of the child-care worker and his functioning with the child, we will refer to certain age differences. It is enough to say only this: Modern psychology has shown that many personality traits have their origins in early childhood. In order to understand the older child, therefore, one often has to go back to the early years. Thus many behavior disturbances in older children may be caused by early childhood experiences. In other words we see life as a continuum, an uninterrupted chain in which all experiences can have an immediate or delayed effect on the personality and the personality adjustment. Therefore, child-care workers who are faced with behavior problems of children always have to look in two directions—what events in the immediate present might have caused the problem, and what experiences in the past might have led to it. Quite often a present event might reactivate feelings from past experiences the child had hidden away. That is why children sometimes react against certain happenings in their present life with inexplicable vehemence, a vehemence which can only be understood if one knows something about their past history. For instance, Johnny, age ten, becomes unbelievably upset when urged to eat food he does not particularly like. He becomes abusive, destructive, and unmanageable. But if one knows that Johnny's mother when he was a small child had used abusive and painful methods to make him eat this food, one can understand his violent reactions.

We know that from the time of his birth a child moves constantly away from parental ties until as an adult he achieves a maximum of independence. From the moment the umbilical cord is severed a child goes through many different phases in the attempt to establish himself as a separate social being. During all this time he needs the constant guidance and protection of his parents, but he needs it in changing forms and degrees. The young child is so dependent on his parents that he is almost completely unable to share the mother with anybody, even those within his own family. This complete dependency changes somewhat as the child becomes more interested in his surroundings and in the other people in his social circle.

The pre-school child can at best tolerate other children, can for short periods play with them, or rather beside them. That is why child welfare workers, doctors, and educators agree that pre-school children should under no circumstances live in an institution. By the age of six a child has usually achieved enough security with his parents and enough interest in other children so that he can attend school with others.

Even the age group between six and ten has a rather difficult time living in groups. While they enjoy certain group activities, their need for individual parental attention is so great that they benefit only in a very limited degree from group living. Only for very cogent reasons should children between six and ten years old be placed in institutions. Child-care workers have to be ready for the many individual demands these children make, for their many individual needs for parental support. There should therefore be adequate child-care staff available for this age group—at least one staff member for four or five children.

Children from ten to thirteen years enjoy group life more perhaps than any other age group. They are full of "lust for life," of the need for motor activity, of adventurous desire to explore their surroundings. They like to do many of these things in small groups, and therefore derive a good deal of satisfaction out of group living at the institution. Nevertheless their primary need is still for parental affection and protection, and their need for individual attention remains very great. Between the many group activities they engage in they have "blue" moods, in which they experience loneliness and homesickness. The moods are heightened in the placed child by romantic fantasies about his parents. Such a child can, therefore, become very wistful or very demanding and resentful. The child-care worker must be ready to engage in many activities with this group and at the same time be the supportive parent figure to the individual child.

Between thirteen and sixteen years, physical development is accompanied by many tensions and confusions. The youngster usually does not yet know how to master his growing body, and all the physiological mysteries surrounding it. All kinds of contrasting emotions overwhelm him at times. He has strong physical urges and a tremendous guilt feeling over these urges, the feeling of being different from everyone else, and the desire for complete immersion into a group of peers. The child may have conviction that he will achieve outstanding success, or complete despair about becoming a "failure." Hyperactivity, inertia, loud rebellion against authority, and passive indifference toward it occur in children of this age. The desire to be approved by members of the other sex is great—and at the same time often denied. Love, with all the sexual tensions and romantic ramifications, occupies a major part of the fantasy life.

Above all, a fluctuating attitude toward parents and parental figures marks this period. Parents are the limiting, coercive, authoritative adversaries of the desired "freedom." At the same time, the adolescent expects his parents to limit him and feels lost and insecure if they do not. A mixture of emotions—love and hate, admiration and disgust, submission and defiance—toward parents, moves the youngster. If he does not live with his own parents, the child often divides his contradictory feelings between his real parents with whom he does not live, and the substitute parents with whom he does. He fantasies all positive feelings toward the real parents and expresses all negative feelings toward the substitute parents. "If I were living with my mother, she would let me stay up until one A.M., but you (the child-care worker) don't understand me."

It is obvious that the role of the child-care worker is very difficult with this age group. Not only is this the age when children normally move away from parental authority, but also they resent a "stranger" assuming such authority. In an institution the negative reaction of individual youngsters is reinforced by the group. Awareness of the dynamics of group living is of special importance in working with this age group. We will discuss this more fully when we talk about group living more specifically. It would be a fallacy to assume that the child of this age does not want the controlling influence of adults. He does indeed but wants it on his own terms. The child-care worker has to be very sure of himself in working with this age group so that he does not counter-react against the youngsters with the same fluctuating feelings which they express toward him. He has to exert controls in a somewhat impersonal way and has to be ready to enter personal relationships with children only as they are ready for it. He has to be sensitive to this readiness. However, with children of this age we can use the group as a means to establish relationships and controls much more advantageously than with those of any other age. While the group heightens certain individual problems of the adolescent, it is at the same time the most important instrument in developing and utilizing their eagerness and capacity to be responsible adults.

Youngsters over sixteen have the same problems in many ways as the group under sixteen. Many of the contrasting feelings are still there. Often, however, there is less vehemence and less abruptness in these contrasts. There is a greater awareness of oncoming adulthood, and more security about themselves. The youngster has emancipated himself sufficiently from the parent so that he does not have to fight constantly for his independence. Although the sailing is by no means smooth yet, and he still fights with his parents, he can tolerate some of their weaknesses without having to contest their total worthwhileness. Similarly parents have usually learned by now to live with the fact that the youngster is a budding adult, and do not need to exert the same amount of parental control. Often the youngster begins to find a more realistic approach to his vocational future. Biological tensions still exist in great strength, but usually the youngster can exercise more self-control in manifesting them. Relationship to the other sex continues to be a major problem. Youngsters at the institution in this age group want to be treated like grown-ups. They feel institutionalization often as an infantilization and resent the rules and regulations as babyish. They particularly want to know why they still need the institution and for how long.

It is important that all children know the reason and the goal of their stay at the institution. For this age group it is imperative. The child-care worker with this age group has to be sensitive to the children's desire to be adults and to their feelings about being in the institution. He is now less of a "parent" but more of a "caretaker"—and a friend. If the individual youngsters decide to invest him with parental qualities, if the "big boys" call Mrs. Brown "Mom Brown," if an individual seeks out the adult as a parent figure, this attitude can be accepted with warmth. It cannot be expected. In this age range as well as in the preceding one the use of the group itself by the child-care worker seems to be the major tool of reaching and managing the youngsters.

What You Should Know about Each Child

How much do child-care workers have to know about a child? How much can the caseworker tell them? Should they read records? Should they know about parents, siblings, IQ's? Should they know when the difficulty started? This question is raised over and over among cottage parents, counselors, children's supervisors, and others who work with children. Often it is accompanied by a certain amount of resentment against the professional staff, or the administration, for not giving enough information about the child. We think there is a clear answer. The child-care workers should know everything about the child that they feel they need to know, everything that enhances their understanding of the child and their ability to handle him. While there is a relationship between knowledge and understanding, information about a child does not necessarily increase one's ability to handle him. More important than detailed knowledge about an individual child is understanding of him. Sensitivity to children's reactions and to one's own is better than accumulated data concerning a particular child. The fact that Mr. Smith, Johnny's father, had been in jail for two months when Johnny was a year old is important only in order to understand that Johnny's present behavior might be influenced by those years. If, after his return to his family Mr. Smith was a good father and he has made up to Johnny the lacks experienced during early childhood, if Johnny shows no marks of this deprivation, this information may not be helpful to the child-care worker at all. On the other hand, should Johnny's father still be involved with the police, or should Johnny still continue to resent his father's past activities, it is necessary for the child-care worker to know this.

> Mary is thirteen years old. She was born out of wedlock to a young woman who, shortly after Mary's birth was committed to a state hospital as an incurable psychotic. The mother is now in a state hospital. When Mary was a year old she was adopted by the Joneses. Years later Mrs. Jones became ill and Mr. Jones was killed in an airplane accident. Mary was placed in a foster home and did not get along there. In another foster home she showed withdrawn, shy, overanxious behavior and refused to go to school. Finally she came to the institution.

How much of this information should be shared with the childcare worker? Everything that is necessary. It is not necessary for the child-care worker to know in what hospital Mary's natural mother is, and what her mother's name is. On the other hand it is necessary for him to know that Mary is an adopted child. If Mary's behavior indicates the possibility of a psychosis it might be necessary for him to know that a psychosis was in her background. Some child-care workers think that they would be better able to handle children if they had more information about them. This is true in many cases. In other cases the child might be handled correctly without the child-care worker's having any specific information. After the war a good number of refugee children, about whom there was no information, came to this country. They were orphans, the sole members of their families to survive the European holocaust. Only long after they arrived in this country could their life histories be pieced together. Sometimes large pieces were missing from the puzzle. Nevertheless, the people who worked with them had to know enough about children and the effects of separation, war, and disturbances on them, in order to understand them. Lack of information made their job more difficult, but it did not make it impossible. More important than knowledge is an attitude of optimism and confidence, ability to understand deviant behavior and to tolerate it, and at the same time ability to set limits notwithstanding sympathetic feelings that the children may evoke. Even the orphan whose parents were killed in the war needs limits; and, on the other hand, even the delinquent who defies his parents needs sympathy and confidence. Without this basic attitude all information is worthless, and often unnecessary. Yet, some basic facts about the child's life are needed and should be readily available.

Should this information be given before the child comes, or while he is in the institution? Should it be given before it is asked for, or after the child-care worker raises specific questions? Again, the answer to this seems rather simple. It should be given when it is needed. A good deal of information is needed before the child comes. His general background, his reasons for coming, the purpose of his stay at the institution, the immediate and the long-time goal of institutional placement should be discussed before the child comes. This should enable the child-care worker to anticipate some of the reactions a child may have in coming to the institution, and also his attitude toward the institution. Did he want to come? Has he friends at the institution? Does he know anyone at the institution? What does he look like? What physical peculiarities does he have, etc.? What kind of behavior can we expect? Does the child wet, stutter, have food fads? If the child-care worker knows these things he can be prepared and can also prepare the children.

In addition to the original data the child-care worker must continue to receive essential information while the child is at the institution, such as changes in his family situation that affect the child, reactions of parents to the institution, medical data, reports about school. All this is relevant to the everyday living of the child. Channels of communication between caseworker, teacher, supervisor, administrator, and child-care workers have to be clearly established so that everyone dealing with the child knows how to handle him best at any given time. This will be discussed more fully in Chapter 7. Equally essential is knowledge about the positives, such as: What can he do well? What are his interests? Does he have any special talents?

Acquiring knowledge about the child is a progressive process, and one which is never finished. Sometimes one learns something which is significant and pertinent about a child's early life long after his admission. Communication of that knowledge is not a one-way street from the caseworker (or other staff) to the child-care workers, but a joint enterprise of all participants in the child's life.

Child-care workers, social workers, teachers, and all those working in child welfare settings have to adhere to the concept of confidentiality. They may not divulge any information given them, either during the time they work at the institution or at any time thereafter. It is the sacred right of every child that any background information about him be respected and guarded. This requires discipline on the part of all members of an institutional staff, lest children's private lives become the subject of gossip and table talk.

While it is not necessary that child-care workers read case records, they ought to have some written information, such as the full name of the child, his birthdate, address of parents, their telephone numbers in case of emergency, all essential health information, and data about school.

Child-care workers wherever possible should make some notes on the children. Their own pertinent observations such as significant reactions regarding adults, children, and visiting parents, should be written down. This not only helps in the exchange of information with caseworkers and supervisors but also represents a vital progress report on the child's adjustment for the child-care worker himself. Unfortunately not enough time is given to child-care workers in most institutions for this kind of record keeping, which could become an essential part of all institutional records. These notes and any other written material on children should be kept safe, so that no unauthorized person (including the child himself) can get to it.

CHAPTER 2

The Children as a Group

Many of the services provided in a children's institution can be given outside, for instance, casework and psychiatric services, medical treatment, special schooling, recreation, and religious education. Even living away from home could be arranged through a foster home. However, the one service that distinguishes an institution most significantly from any other form of care is group living—the living together of children in a group rather than in a family unit. Indeed, group living is the major specific purpose of institutionalization and together with the element of protection of the child from the dangers within himself and within his society, is the most cogent reason for the existence of institutions.

The people in charge of the group living process, the child-care workers, are indeed the guardian angels, the hub of the wheel of institutional care. They make the process of group living an integrated constructive part of the total program. If they cannot do this, institutionalized living becomes futile and loses its major purpose.

We must, therefore, investigate what constitutes a living group in the institution, and what distinguishes it from other forms of communal living such as the family.

A strange and almost miraculous thing happens in some institutional groups, where it might be least expected—i.e., where there are children who had been cast out from any previous group. They had been pariahs in their peer groups, rejected by their families, and isolates in school. In the institution we expect this aggregate of asocial, lonely, and rugged individualists to form social groups, to stick together, abide by rules, regulations and standards, to establish positive relationships among themselves. Is it not rather unrealistic, contradictory to all logic, to expect that these children who have proven to have so little group potential could become a group? Yet strange and illogical as it might seem, it does happen. After a while they really do form a group. Often, indeed, this group formation becomes their most important tie to institutional life. This is all the more astonishing since most of these children come against their will. They have been sent here by their parents, by courts, social agencies, or sometimes their schools. Even if they verbalize that they wanted to come, they did not really want to. No sooner are they at the institution than homesickness sets in. Their desire to return to their own homes, and their fantasies about their homes let them forget their real reasons for coming.

Nevertheless the group process does affect and envelop most of them. What in particular can the child-care worker do to make this group process so effective that it represents a true value in their lives, a new and important experience, from which they get new strength? How can we help them utilize the group process as a partial substitute for family living? How can we use it to prepare children for a future life in a family, in the community, and with their peers? How can we make it an experience which they will remember as positive all their lives? In the following pages some of these questions will be examined. The basic ingredients that make up group life will be investigated. Some of the dynamics that determine interrelationships between children and adults in an institutional group will be analyzed.

Some Basic Concepts

THE COMMUNITY OF EXPERIENCES

Even though they meet as total strangers, children who live together in a group twenty-four hours a day are linked by a multitude of joint experiences. They arise at approximately the same time, have their meals together, share many recreational activities, have the same clothing routines, the same physical hygiene standards, the same health procedures. Many of them go to school together, share chores in the household, receive similar allowances, and share other such experiences.

Even if they resist interaction they cannot avoid looking at each other's faces. It is important that common experiences be used to aid group formation wherever possible. Here the child-care worker has an important role. While each child must remain an individual, and while uniform regulations for each child are not recommended by any means, many of these daily experiences can make group events. The chapter on the twenty-four hours of the day will discuss these experiences. Work, as well as play, can become a common experience for children. Each chore of the day is not only a task that must be done, but also an opportunity for the children to do it together. If they like these tasks it will bring them closer to each other, and to the adult who supervises them. Attempts should always be made to make common tasks as palatable to children as possible. Even if they do not like a task it may still strengthen the bond between them. They carry together the "yoke" imposed by the adult. This strengthening of the common bond, as long as the results can be controlled, has a very positive meaning to children, although it is sometimes difficult for adults.

The child's experiences in an institution are more or less regular. It has often been said, and it is almost true, that the child's day in the institution is over-scheduled. While excesses of scheduling are damaging and to be regretted, the child derives benefits from scheduling. Children who come to the institution have often lived in an emotionally and socially disorganized environment where events and people were unpredictable, where the order of living was often interrupted by personal needs of the people who made up the environment. The institutional environment is relatively well regulated. Events in the institution are quite predictable. One is awakened at a certain time in the morning. The child does not have to worry during the night about whether he will oversleep and miss his classes. He does not have to worry during school time whether someone is home after school, or whether meals will be served at the regular hours. He knows, for example, that the homework period will be from six to seven, and activities from seven to eight. There will be a snack before bedtime, and finally, whether one likes it or not, there will be bedtime. Even in going to bed, established procedures are observed. This regularity (which must not be confused with rigidity) not only represents security to the individual child, but is an important group value. The children know that for part of the day they have to be together. Even the shy child who likes to hide knows that at certain times he has to be with the group. Even the "bully" who likes to run his own show has to submit to this regularity like anyone else.

Giving children the same schedule establishes a comparable frame of reference and a secure reality for them. This regularity, being universal and impersonal, minimizes the danger of an individual child feeling discriminated against, and helps create an order to which the whole group has to submit. The organization of time thus helps create some order in the life of the individual and thus leads to group feeling.

VOLUNTARY AND COMPULSORY GROUP PARTICIPATION

It would be fallacious to expect children in a group to enjoy being together all the time, nor would this be desirable. When we think back on our family lives, we think of a few incidents, perhaps, that made the family a group. We might think of a Sunday meal, or of the walk to church together, or of the daily dinner. We have a tendency to forget certain unpleasant experiences, such as when we wanted to be away from the group and do something different from the rest of the family, when we used every opportunity to get away. Sometimes this might have been on a Sunday afternoon when relatives visited, or during an evening meal when we had to wait until everyone finished while our friends were waiting outside for us, or when we wanted to listen to our favorite radio program and father wanted to listen to the news. There are many involuntary experiences even in a normal family group. These are matched by a number of voluntary ones. This balance of voluntary and compulsory participation makes group life in the family possible, acceptable, and basically enjoyable.

Even seemingly completely voluntary groups can become compulsory by the mere length of the group experiences. If we take a group of boys and have them play a game which lasts too long, we find after a while that a few boys drop out. Another few may stay in the game because of group pressure rather than free will. We know of children who want pets, promise to take care of them, and then refuse to do so. A baseball game, a meal, a play rehearsal, or an outing, anything that lasts beyond the impetus of the original voluntary motivation, can become an unpleasant compulsory chore.

This is even more so with chores that are originally not voluntary. Group living in an institution is itself an involuntary experience. Children do not come to us by choice. In a way the total twenty-four hours of the day are a compulsory commitment. Children often resent activities at the institution which they previously liked because they have the feeling that everything is forced upon them and that they are the victims of adult coercion. It is important to give them the feeling in the course of their stay at the institution that they have some measure of self determination. Many activities lend themselves to such voluntary participation.

There are some basic activities in which the child must participate whether he wants to or not, such as going to bed, getting up, physical hygiene, showering, and going to school. There are many areas where the group can have a choice. Thus within the balanced diet of a weekly menu it might be possible to arrange for certain preferred foods. Broccoli could replace spinach. One could even imagine a whole generation of children in an institution being brought up without spinach if its elimination would help the group spirit. In some group living units children may do their beds after breakfast, while in others they may do them before breakfast. While on some occasions some schedules are dictated by necessity, they can usually be modified. Often they are based on arbitrary decisions of the person in charge of the unit. The child-care worker has an opportunity to utilize voluntary participation in planning innumerable events provided that the secure structure and the basic regularity of daily living are not jeopardized. To be sure, some new children, especially hostile children, do not accept anything voluntarily, refuse to participate in making decisions, and do everything in their power to make decisions seem compulsory dictates. Somewhat better adjusted children, however, will welcome such participation which will help them in their growth and treatment. It helps them above all to accept the many compulsory aspects of group living more readily and with less hostility.

Many compulsory aspects of institutional living have therapeutic, educational, and group-formative functions. Adult insistence on observing rules show the children that they want and are able to direct them in socially acceptable patterns. One of children's basic needs, the need to be directed, is met by many of these compulsory activities. Even though a child might voice resistance about an unpleasant task, he has enough social awareness to know that these tasks should be done. If he does not do them he feels inadequate and guilty. The adult's insistence on task fulfillment prevents these guilt feelings. Children feel safe and protected in such a structure. Basically they resent an adult who lets them "get away with murder" more than one who sets limits too narrowly. The child who complains that "they make me go to school" and that "those tyrants make me comb my hair," has not only feelings of anger and rebellion against the adult world but also the feeling that "they are stronger than me. They will not let me become delinquent or neglected." In an institutional group many children have this feeling. They rebel together against the adult "dictatorship." A good deal of energy is used in this rebellion, a good deal of aggression spent. Yet, this aggression toward adults reduces their hostility toward each other, indeed binds youngsters closer together. Since underneath this aggression toward the adult is the feeling that the adult is right, the whole group feels that the institution is strong and orderly, and each child feels not only the bond of common "servitude" but also the bond of being commonly protected and controlled. There are innumerable voluntary aspects to group living. Some of them are practiced often unbeknown to children and adults. In most institutions children may choose to speak to the adult or not, to read a book, play the radio, collect stamps, etc. In all of these voluntary activities the adult can be a helping person, making children aware of the possibilities of choice within the regulated structure, offering them a variety of choices, allowing them to see that they have some part in con-

trolling their program. The more voluntary participation is possible for a child, the better the prospects of making his institutional
stay successful.

The child-care worker should therefore utilize all channels of
voluntary and free participation with the group. He can, on the
other hand, feel assured that his insistence on fulfillment of obliga-
tory tasks is just as important for the children.

THE DURATION OF GROUP EMOTIONS

It has been mentioned above that every group experience is basically short. Human beings are different from one another. The
feeling of being alike, belonging together, and being united, is
of short duration. The longing for friendships, for love, for belonging to a cause, and the search for union with other people accom-
panies human beings all their lives, but the moments in which
they feel that they are totally united and do belong with others
are of short duration. Yet these moments are strong, electrifying
and binding enough for human beings to want to experience them
again and again. These feelings motivate them to arrange their
lives so that, in spite of their differences, they can live and work
with others. They make compromises with their shortcomings in
order to achieve moments of togetherness and belonging. This is
true in marriage, work, religion, social and political affiliations,
and many other activities. The same is true of children in an institution. The real, intense feeling of belonging together is a rare
and short one. Many group experiences are needed to give them
this feeling. Many a game is played without ever giving them this
feeling; many a party goes by without it. Then suddenly it happens, seemingly unexpected—at mealtime, at a story hour around
the fireplace, at a birthday party or a Christmas celebration. The
children seem not only to participate in it but to become a part of
it. They seem to say: "This is good. Life is fun." It would be
foolish to expect that all group events could lend themselves to
such deep emotional experiences. Indeed, it would be impossible
to live at such a high pitch. Yet, in a sense every voluntary group
activity should carry the potential for such an experience, and the

child-care worker has to do his part to bring it about. For it does not come about quite as spontaneously as it would seem. The stage—so to speak—has to be set for it.

Receptivity on the part of the participants has to be stimulated. The elements of freedom and dignity, of spontaneity and planning, have to be construed to this end. The timing of the event has to be just right in order to bring about the experience. The experience itself should be short, impressive and genuine, and should meet the children's interest and emotions at this time. It must be concluded shortly after its high point is reached, for length kills it.

Some children go through institutional life without ever having had such experiences, others do not have enough of them. In some institutions the responsible staff assumes that such deep group experiences can be turned on and off like a faucet, and so fill the children with over-staged adult inspired pseudo-emotional experiences which fail to mean anything to them. The child-care worker who is fortunate and skilled enough to utilize group activities occasionally for a real group experience has not only given the children a deep and significant creative experience from which they can benefit, but has at the same time established a bond among them. In creating this group bond he establishes himself as a part of it. This will have a continuing beneficial effect on group activity tasks.

PRIVACY

Children not only are not capable of experiencing this group bond often, but have a limited capacity for group experiences of any kind. Above everything else every child is a private individual. More often than not the average child has neither desire nor ability to participate in group activities of any kind. Institutions have to be aware of this. Children living together feel exposed and exhibited not only to adults but also to each other. In some institutions not even the toilets provide privacy. Children often resent this exposure as degrading and showing lack of respect for their individual dignity. Withdrawal from the group, loafing, self-imposed isolation or even moroseness are by no means always signs of pathology. On the contrary, they are often the healthy reaction of a child who fights to retain his individuality and personal dignity. The institutional program has to take this need into consideration. The child-care worker has to make possible not only group experiences, but also privacy. The daily program must include periods without any scheduled group activities. Living quarters must allow for withdrawal of an individual child from the group. There must be enough staff coverage to permit such privacy without limiting group activities. Only if the children feel that a certain privacy is guaranteed them, can they ever voluntarily participate in group activities. That is why this note on privacy belongs here where we talk about the use of the group experience as a growth-promoting tool.

THE GROUP CODE

The child-care worker has to be familiar with the rules and regulations of the institution. He has to know what is expected of him, what is allowed and what forbidden, which rules are definitely set and which can be modified as the situation requires. Some institutions have established manuals for their child-care workers which give them the major rules and regulations in writing. Yet even with a highly effective system of recorded communication there are still many "unwritten laws" which just cannot all be officially transmitted, but have to be learned in practice.

There is another set of "rules" which are never recorded, indeed, which are not even recognized as rules. These are the rules which the children create themselves. They are not recorded and often are not even consciously known to the children. However, they are very powerful laws and often determine an individual child's happiness and acceptance within the group.

In every group of children over nine years of age there exists a group code, an unspoken set of rules of fair play by which they evaluate their deeds and misdeeds. This group code is quite different from the adult code. In an adolescent boys' cottage, for instance, the first ten commandments of group code may read as follows: (1) Playing truant is allowed, but not taking a younger child along on a truancy escapade. (2) Stealing from adults is allowed, but not stealing from other children. (3) It is strictly forbidden to "snitch" (tell) on another child, except if he is new or group-rejected. (4) Cursing is allowed, but not cursing involving parents. (5) Sneaking out at night is allowed, especially to a girls' cottage, but raiding a cottage of younger children at night is not. (6) Teasing another child about his parents' inadequacy is forbidden. (7) Teasing another child about physical handicaps is forbidden, but teasing him about psychological handicaps is not. (8) Do not trust adults in power, especially new ones. (9) Gripe loudly about unpleasant things at the institution, but withhold praise of good things. (10) Whatever you do, don't get caught.

In other age groups another group code is in operation. The six-to ten-year-old group, for instance, allow "snitching," which could well be another indication that they are not ready for group living. Among girls, a definite code exists regarding sex behavior.

It is obvious that many things forbidden by the adult code are allowed by the group code, and many things forbidden by the group code are permitted or encouraged by adults. The child who commits an act in violation of the rules of the institution is censured by the group only if this act happens to be in violation of the group code. The group will usually criticize a child who steals from other children, but may be indifferent to a child's stealing from adults. If the child-care worker tries to get the group's cooperation in finding out who stole from an adult, he is likely to meet with passive resistance.

One of the jobs of the child-care worker new to the group is to find out what the group code is. This is a hard assignment, because there are no obvious, clear-cut methods of learning it. It requires curiosity, sensitivity, and capacity for dispassionate observation. New children, who are not handicapped in this area by their own set of values, have an advantage over new staff members. They find out in an amazingly short time the do's and don't's of the group. Even unintelligent children often have an uncanny gift for sizing up the group and its code. The children who do not find out remain "isolates." Next to getting to know the group code the child-care worker's problem is, of course, handling the discrepancies between the group code and the adult code in cases of misbehavior. This is one of the most serious problems in discipline and will be discussed under that topic. The child-care worker has to insist on conformity to adult rules. His job is made easier if he knows in what relation these rules stand to the group code. If they conflict he must be aware of the resistance he will meet to any corrective measures, not only from the individuals involved in the infraction of the rules, but also from group leaders.

One of the most difficult jobs of a child-care worker is modification of the group code itself. Nevertheless, this is often necessary. It is a long-range project which cannot be achieved over night. A good relationship to the group, personal security and intensive work with group leaders are necessary to bring this about. The group must be convinced that such a change is for their (and not only for the adult's) benefit. They must know that the adult does not want to "take over" or "'suppress" their right to their own group value system, but really has a deep understanding of it.

It is, of course, sometimes necessary to suppress the group code if it conflicts with the child's basic needs. The need for protection supersedes all other considerations. If suppression has to be used it should be done wisely and effectively. If the child-care worker knows that this is the only means open to him at this particular time he must act without wavering and hesitation. However, he might as well know that the children will regard his action as suppression and that the leaders of the group will try in every way to undermine his power.

The child-care worker must understand these basic concepts of group living if he is to play the important role with the youngsters that his assignment implies. He must understand them to play his part in the group living process.

The Dynamics of Group Living

Family relationships are based on the interaction of father, mother, and children. The foundation for family relationship is formed before the child is born, in the relationship between husband and wife. If their relationship is satisfactory the chances are good that the relationship between them and the children, and of the children to each other will also be satisfactory. The diagram of a family of three looks like a triangle with the father and mother at the base. The diagram of a family with several children looks like a series of triangles with the same base with interconnecting lines at the apexes.

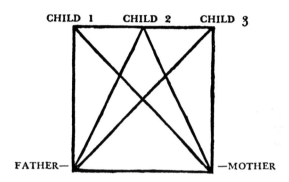

No matter how strong the relationship between siblings is, the relationship between parents is the most essential one. Father and mother determine the patterns of living: the educational, cultural, religious, and recreational orientation. The content of the child's life depends on the content of the parents' life. Let us look at just one aspect: conversation around a dinner table. Children in a family hear conversation which concerns the whole family. In a family things are geared partly to the children, and partly to the adults. Children hear about taxes as well as about the circus which has just come to town. The father might come home depressed one evening and talk about his job troubles or his political activities. The children are expected to adjust to this adult pattern of family living, while the parents at the same time try to make concessions to the children's need in the planning of the family life.

It is quite different in a group living situation. Here the adults alone do not form the base of the living pattern. Children in an institution seldom hear about the child-care worker's worries about his tax bills or doctor bills, or his interest in politics. The whole program is child-centered, and because of the institution's functions, different from real life. However, since children in institutions usually have little ability to tolerate, identify with, and participate in the problems of others, it is important that the living pattern be child-centered.

A diagram of a children's group would not appear as a triangle, but as a system of concentric circles.

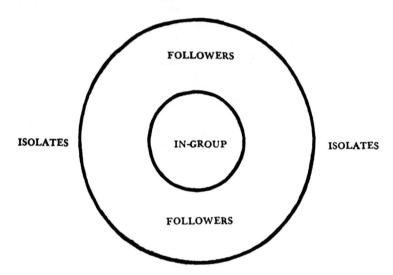

In the center of these circles is the "in-group." These are leaders of the group. Usually there are two or three children in a group of about fifteen whose approval is sought by everyone, and whose influence is felt on program, group values, and group interaction. If they approve of a new child-care worker or of a new child, the group usually will accept these new people.

Around the leaders are the followers. Often there are several cliques of followers affiliated to each other in different degrees of closeness. There may be three or four such cliques in a living unit.

At times the in-group accepts into their midst one of the followers, who then becomes a member of the in-group itself. Sometimes the leadership, through discharge from the unit or withdrawal of one member, disintegrates. Then one of the cliques takes over the leadership. Or at another time there is a struggle for leadership between two groups, and one clique deposes the in-group and itself assumes the in-group role.

On the extreme outside of this diagram we find the isolates. These are children not accepted by any of the cliques or the in-group. There are three different types of isolates, the new child, the withdrawn child, and the group-rejected child.

The success of group living depends on the movement from the state of isolation to the in-group, or as far towards the in-group as possible and on the speed of this movement. The group is in constant flux. Leaders change, cliques change, the in-group changes, and the isolates change. While this constant movement creates many factors of instability, it also represents the dynamic life of the group. Children sense this movement quite often better than the adults. They are aware whether a child is "in" or "out." In order to understand this process and the role of the child-care worker in these interrelationships let us look more specifically at the leader, the follower, and the isolate.

The Leaders (the In-Group)

In trying to understand why certain children develop leadership roles in a group, and to appreciate these roles, the child-care worker has to be quite objective in looking at the leaders. This is difficult because nothing represents a greater threat to the child-care worker than the group leader. Child-care workers in an institution very often have an emotional reaction to leadership which prevents them from appreciating all the energy, intelligence, and ability to identify with others that are inherent in group leadership.

The leader in an institutional group has certain qualities which make it possible for him to be a leader. He knows the group. He knows what they want and what they don't want, when they want it, and under what conditions. This knowledge is not intellectually acquired. It is something which the youngster senses, though he may not even be conscious of it.

John, a would-be leader of a group of twelve-year-olds, complained about Michael's "dictatorial" leadership. On Saturday morning the child-care worker asked both boys for suggestions for the afternoon's program. John wanted to go roller skating, but he did not know what the other boys wanted to do. Michael, on the other hand, said casually that three of them (naming the children, one of them John) wanted to go roller skating, and four boys (including himself) wanted to go bike riding, three probably wanted to go swimming, while three did not want to go anywhere. "We will go bike riding—at least most of us," he added challengingly. This is what most of them did with their counselor, except John, who held out for roller skating.

John did not know what the group wanted. He was much too self-interested and rigid to understand and identify with the wishes of the group.

Usually the leader has skills which the group desires. These skills and interests may be somewhat above the group's performance level, but are never so far ahead that the children cannot comfortably participate in this activity with their leader. He gets enough fun out of his group acceptable interests, and out of the activities in which the group can participate. When he no longer gets enough fun out of them he will not remain the leader. He might actually become an isolate because he has outgrown the group.

Martin was one of three boys who formed the in-group in cottage number one. He had many more interests than the other children, and was more skilled in many respects. He enjoyed playing with others, participating with them in games, and organizing their activities. However, after about a half year Martin's interests in more adolescent activities became very obvious. He spent much time at the baseball field with older boys of another cottage, and often asked one of the cottage counselors to play chess with him because the other children "don't know how to play." He complained about bedtime and said, "They treat us like babies. We have to go to bed an hour earlier than cottage number three." Soon Martin found that the other two boys of the in-group did not include him any more in their planning and that he was more alone. The child-care worker then recommended that it was time to move Martin into the next older cottage group, which was done. After a few months he was a member of the in-group in his new cottage.

In a way the leader has the ability to identify with others, to see beyond himself and to incorporate other children's interests in his own. A leader may be selfish. He may exert a domineering influence—but he is not self-centered to the point that he cannot

see the interests of the others, their abilities, and their readiness
to follow him and to obey the group code.

No other quality of the leader is so important as courage.
Personal courage, or "guts," as the children call it, is necessary
because he expresses in words and action certain thoughts which
the children would like to but don't dare express. In a way he
formulates what everyone feels but does not express, or is perhaps
not even able to formulate. Most of the time this demonstration of
courage is an expression of hostility to the adults. Children admire
the leader because he can express hostility where they are afraid
to do so.

> The cottage mother came in with a new permanent wave. Most of the
> girls expressed mild and polite approval of her new hairdo. Sonya
> expressed enthusiasm for it, but she was always enthusiastic about
> everything. Annette and Sylvia, the leaders of the group, were not
> around at this time. Later, as they looked over the new hairdo,
> Annette said, "Now you even *look* like a witch." This cottage mother
> was not well liked by the children. Her rather angular features were
> indeed accentuated by the new hairdo. For a moment the children
> were taken aback and remained silent. The hairdo was wholly re-
> jected. Unfortunately the cottage mother then acquired the unpleas-
> ant nickname of "the witch," which she did not lose when she changed
> her hairdo again in a few weeks. The hairdo was only an incidental
> opportunity for Annette to express something the whole cottage had
> felt.

The leader's ability to express the group's underlying feeling is
often painful and annoying to the child-care worker. But it is also
a sign of the child's capacity to observe and formulate, and of his
courage in expressing his thoughts. This ability and courage,
directed into more constructive and socially acceptable channels,
are very desirable character traits.

Another quality of the leader is fairness within the group code.
This does not mean fairness by staff standards, but by the children's
standards. Leaders see to it that the group code is obeyed; this is
their major instrument for controlling the group. They are zeal-
ously watchful that the children pay as much attention to the
group code as to the rules set up by the adults. Many groups have

established procedures which are unsound, damaging, and unacceptable to the adults, and adults have to interfere with them. Such procedures as initiation rites for newcomers, "hell week," are frightening, sadistic traditions which cannot be tolerated. The leaders usually perpetuate such procedures and rites. The child-care worker must take action against these activities and thereby antagonize the leaders. At this point the leaders attack the child-care worker's interference as "unfair," and both group and leaders will become "traditional" and "conservative" and insist that group traditions be maintained.

Sometimes adults tend to give in to the leaders about such issues, accepting certain activities such as initiation, group punishment, or group jokes on one child, with the rationale that it is done in colleges, in the army, and in fraternal organizations. This does not make it sound, particularly in view of these children's problems. Yet the child-care worker's role in this is sometimes not so difficult as it seems. The leader's sense of fairness within the code is based on his ability to recognize that there must be fairness for everyone. If the group action is really unfair to some child, the leader's sense of fairness can be mobilized to become a source of support for the adult's position.

Work with leaders, therefore, becomes a crucial task of the child-care worker. If he does not know how to handle leaders, if his relationship with them is one of antagonism and suspicion, his job becomes difficult, and his influence on the group is reduced. Child-care workers are often guilty of two mistakes. They try to make puppets of the leaders. They would like leaders to use their influence on the group to carry out a part of their own functions. They make them junior assistant administrators. When leaders take over such roles they lose their powers in the group within a short time.

> For instance, if the children do not switch off the lights on time, the child-care worker might say to a leader, "Johnny, I assign you to see that all lights are out at nine o'clock." Johnny, being ambitious and having a great desire to dominate, and to be respected by adults, might accept such an assignment, or he might be forced to do so. When Johnny must go around and switch off the lights and possibly

report those children who do not turn off their lights on time, he takes over functions which the children expect an adult to carry. As a result, the children feel that he cannot be trusted, that he is a "stooge." He won't be "in" with the children any more. They will not tell him their plans for pranks, delinquent activities, or running away. If they do, Johnny will be thrown into conflict because he must become a traitor either to the children or to the trusting adult.

The leadership process and the dynamics of group living are interrupted, temporarily at least. After a while Johnny either feels isolated or resigns from this imposed office. He might then even outdo other children in some of their delinquent activities in order to regain their confidence. The child-care worker will be especially disappointed in Johnny and unable to understand "what got into him." Or Johnny might use his adult-supported power sadistically to exert more control over the group, and become hated and feared by the children. In this case too he has lost his indigenous leadership.

Another mistake child-care workers often make is competing with leaders. There is no question that leaders consciously or unconsciously compete with the child-care worker. The insistence on abiding by the group code is an act of competition. Often, however, the adult also tries to compete with the in-group, to outsmart the leaders, to show them that they are "not so hot" themselves, and to wean other children away from the leaders. He might ridicule the leaders, challenge their authority, or minimize their achievements. The child-care worker forgets in such situations that he is an adult and the children are children. In an institution all children—leaders, followers, and isolates—have many problems with which they must be helped. One of their major needs is that the ego remain intact and be strengthened. Their self-confidence must also be strengthened.

The child-care worker is left out of the diagram of the group because he is not really a part of it. The child-care worker stimulates, enables the group process to take place, helps leadership to develop, recognizes the potentialities for leadership and guides the constant, dynamic interaction that makes group living an educationally and therapeutically helpful process. The leader of a group of thirteen-year-olds might tell a somewhat off-color joke. The children might like the joke and the child-care worker might not. Would the child-care worker then tell another story to better the one of the leader? He certainly would not. This would thus exert more pressure on the leader to tell an even more questionable joke in order to compete. The child-care worker might find himself in a vicious circle of competition which would help no one. The following case serves as an example of a child-care worker's competing with a leader.

A cottage mother tried to rehearse a play with the children for a campus-wide affair. Once a month every cottage presented some entertainment at an assembly of the institution. On February 18 it was the turn of cottage number seven. Steven was the uncontested leader in this cottage. He had a lot of ideas and was creative, but was quite hostile to adults. He identified well with the group, knew what the group could do, and what they were not able to do. Since February 18 fell between Lincoln's and Washington's birthdays, Mrs. Brown felt that it was fitting to have a play on Lincoln or Washington, or both, and indeed she discovered in the school library a play in which Lincoln and Washington met in Heaven and had a patriotic discussion. Steve had indicated that he did not want any "patriotic stuff." However, it happened that just before the final decision on the play was made he became ill and had to spend two weeks in the infirmary. During this time Mrs. Brown persuaded the reluctant group to prepare for this play. The major parts were given to isolates rather than to leaders. Mrs. Brown felt that this was good since the isolates "never get a chance." She made a tremendous personal investment in this play, helped the children with their lines and costumes, and exhausted herself with daily rehearsals to which the children came with very little enthusiasm. Three days before the play was to be given Steve returned to the cottage and listened to the rehearsals. His verdict was "it stinks." Immediately almost all the children agreed with him, refused to continue the Lincoln-Washington play and suddenly "forgot" their lines. Steve then suggested that they make up a mystery play and the whole group was enthusiastic. Within three days the group wrote, rehearsed and played a five-act mystery about "The Death of Mrs. Schnabelofsky," in which there was a lot of shooting, and in which everyone but Steve was killed in the end.

Mrs. Brown was disappointed about this. She asked for assistance from her supervisor. He arranged that some of the songs of the original Lincoln-Washington play be sung, and some of the costumes worn on this occasion. He did this mainly because he felt sorry for Mrs. Brown, who felt all her efforts were a total loss. Mrs. Brown had really misunderstood the group interrelationship and especially the leadership role of Steven. She actually competed with Steven and admitted in a supervisory conference that while she regretted Steven's illness, she was relieved that he was out of the group during this time, because it gave her a free hand with the children.

Instead of trying to weaken a child's leadership qualities it is important to recognize them. More than anyone else, the child-care worker must give the leader the feeling that he understands his desire to lead, and his underlying hostility toward the institution. It is equally important that the child-care worker not be afraid of the leader. Often the recognition which the leader receives from the group distorts his own concepts of reality, and he thinks people really have to respect him and be afraid of him. The child-care worker has to express his questions about the leader's activities if he disagrees with them. He must contradict, reprimand, censure, and discipline the leader as readily as he does others; but he must avoid being especially punitive to him, to outdo or undo him as leader.

It is advisable that a child-care worker, when preparing a program, anticipate how the leadership will take to it. He might use leaders as a sounding board for the group's readiness. A casual remark: "Do you have any idea as to what we could do for Johnny's birthday party?" or, "Do you think we should change the bedroom arrangement?" might serve to get the leader's reaction as a barometer for the group's attitude. If there is great resistance he might want to delay the planned activity. At least he is prepared for opposition and can take steps to meet it wisely. Very often it is possible to drop an idea in a child's mind and have it develop in him so that it becomes his own. Ideas and suggestions made by leaders are more readily carried out by children. There are many areas of group living in which children can be asked to make decisions. For instance, many recreational activities can be determined by the group. They must know clearly the limitations of their authority in making decisions. Children can choose freely within these limits, and leaders can exert their influence readily in these activities. It is important that these limitations be clearly established, so that the children do not over-estimate the limits of their authority. For instance, if one lets them choose the type of birthday party for Johnny, they might decide on an all-night affair with expensive dishes and a well known band. If the child-care worker has to reject their decision he takes away the authority he gave them originally. If, on the other hand, the child-care worker, while inviting them to prepare the party, stipulates the amount of money available and the hours in which it can be held, the children will not be disappointed afterwards.

While recreational activities lend themselves well to utilization of the in-group, leadership usually expresses itself in grievances against the adult rather than in program planning for the group. The child-care worker's handling of grievances is, therefore, an important part of his job. It is expected that in a twenty-four-hour living situation many occasions arise in which the children feel that they are treated unfairly. Whether this is true or not is actually not so relevant as the way in which the children react. They feel that another injustice has been done them, and that the adult world does not care enough. It is therefore important to give attention to any grievance of the children. It is natural that the leaders are most vocal about these complaints. For instance, a leader may complain that the food is not good. Whether this complaint is valid, untrue, or exaggerated, the child-care worker should be seriously interested in the children's grievance and allow them to discuss it without becoming a party for or against it. He can show them that he is interested in their welfare, support their right to complain, and indicate ways in which they can most effectively deal with this complaint. He might tell them that he will discuss this with the dietician or the administration. He might arrange for a delegation of the group to see the dietician or the director of the institution. The children then have the feeling that they are understood rather than rebuffed, appreciated rather than ignored. Thus, instead of fighting the leaders who act as the group's voice he helps them to work the grievances through in an organized way and use their leadership qualities to improve the institution. If they can bring about an improvement they feel that their leadership has brought constructive results. The child-care worker has helped them to move from rebellious complaining into organized, constructive group action. The gripers have become planners, and they can be more easily helped to see the world and themselves in a more hopeful light.

One of the most frequent complaints of leaders is, "there is nothing to do"—in spite of the fact that the institution has a well-equipped and full schedule of activities, more than are available to the child in his own family or community. If the child-care worker tries to deny the child's complaint, or to combat it by suggesting more activities, or even by acquiring more equipment, he does not understand the underlying motivation of the complaint. What the children are really saying is: "Something is missing in our group life. We do not get enough fun out of being together. We want something more exciting. We have not had a group activity that was a real group experience and gave us the feeling of belonging together." The child-care worker can help children express some of these feelings. He can then guide them into discussing why this came about, and what might be done about it. Maybe group activities did not meet the children's interest. Perhaps they did not involve enough children, or the child-care worker himself did not participate enough. Out of such discussion can come planning of more appropriate activities. This is another opportunity for the in-group to do some constructive planning and organization, and to use their leadership abilities in a positive rather than a negative way.

However, even if such a change in orientation cannot be brought about, even if the leaders remain negativistic and demanding—the child-care worker's calm interest and understanding of their demands will in the long run lower their hostility and aggressiveness.

The Followers

Most children in a group living unit are followers. Many followers have all the aspirations to leadership, but usually do not have the ability to identify sufficiently with other children. They are too preoccupied with themselves, too insecure to identify freely with the group. Only as they overcome this insecurity can they assume leadership. Most lacking in followers is the courage to deviate from the group and to express their own opinions, which, as we saw, is the unexpressed group opinion. This courage is given to only a few.

The followers, therefore, are more anxious to be like the group than to be unique. They are more anxious to be accepted by the majority, especially the leaders, than to express their own individuality. Often the followers experience confusion in finding out what the group norm and the group code are, who the leaders are, whose word is important, with whom it is important to be on good terms, with whom one can be aggressive and with whom submissive. Knowledge of the structure and the social pattern of the group must be acquired by everyone in the group. Most children acquire it rather easily. This proves that, in spite of their problems, their adjustment to reality is sufficiently intact that they are able to readily assess the facts of group life. It means that this part of their egos, even though they might be otherwise very destructive, is intact. They not only recognize the group reality, but also have the ability to adjust to it.

The relationship of the follower to the leader is an ambivalent one. It is not just acceptance for there are undercurrents of anger, hostility and jealousy. This jealousy often comes into the open and at times leads to an interesting and painful struggle for leadership. The would-be leader, a follower who possesses the courage but not the other qualifications, especially knowledge of the group, will wait for the moment of leadership weakening in order to "take over." There are moments in which he really seems to succeed in taking over the group through some rebellion against the adult or through a special skill which puts him in the limelight. However, this leadership usually does not last. Either new leader groups develop, or the old in-group recovers and the would-be leader is mercilessly put back in his place.

Other followers' feelings towards the leader are also ambivalent. While they submit to him they resent him because he represents the strong person they would like to be. He represents an older brother or perhaps a father person, a self chosen father person whom they admire and resent at the same time. This ambivalence and hostility is usually less focused when there is not one leader but an in-group of two or three who seem to work closely with each other. While the direct hostility is not so great, the feeling of exclusion might seem greater because the leaders are self sufficient and do not seem to need their followers.

Cliques and Sub-Group Formations

While the leadership group is the most dominant group in the living unit, followers form their own sub-groups, or cliques, as we shall call them for the purpose of this discussion. Two, three, or four children band together. They play together, walk together to and from school, want to have the same bedroom, sit around the dining room table together, and tend to be with each other in recreational activities. Most significantly, they always share secrets with each other. In younger groups they often communicate with each other in special language, a secret code which binds them together. This code often concerns common sexual interests, and is full of symbolic terms and signs which are supposedly understood only by them. Sometimes the secret concerns delinquent activities, such as plans to sneak out together at night, raid the icebox, steal in the five-and-ten-cent store. It is the secret knowledge about each other and the sharing of the secret with each other, which gives other children the feeling of being left out. This gives the clique a feeling of their own power and softens the pain of being excluded by the leaders. It is again interesting to observe that children up to eight years do not usually have the strength to keep a secret, and therefore, will reveal their "secret" to others, thereby jeopardizing the basis for the clique formation, and consequently the group living process itself. This is further evidence—if it is needed—that young children are not ready for group living.

Even in the older group at times their "secrets" are not really secret. As a matter of fact nearly every one knows about them, and many cliques have the same secrets. However, as far as the children are concerned it remains their identification badge and loses its power only when shared openly with outsiders.

> Three thirteen-year-old boys from cottage number five had made arrangements to get up at midnight, go outside and catch frogs. The preparation for this adventure was a very important experience for them, and the boisterous and demonstrative "secrecy" which surrounded it was amusing and pathetic. The cottage parents noticed the preparation, knew something was up, and were on the alert during the night, and so caught the boys in the act. This, however, did not affect their clique formation. On the contrary, it probably strengthened it. Now they not only had a secret together, they were in trouble together. However, a few weeks later this same group of children planned to break in the storeroom of the institution in the early evening hour while other children were engaged in activities. When they came to the storeroom they found two other boys from the cottage engaged in the same activity. This really was a big blow to their clique formation. They either had the choice of accepting the other children in their clique thus making it an unwieldy group or giving up their clique altogether. A few days later one child of the group of three attached himself very closely to the other two boys and a new clique formation developed.

Frequently the members of a clique are eager to share their secret with the leaders. They offer it, so to speak, as a bribe. They may inform the leaders ahead of time that they plan to run away, or to sneak out at night. They would like to get the approval or even the participation of the leaders. Very often the leaders discard or reject their overtures rather casually or even brutally. Usually they keep themselves above the clique activities, but magnanimously approve of them. While the "common secret" is the most significant criterion for clique formation and friendship sub-groups, it is by no means the only one. There is the communion of interests which bind children together: common hobbies, common skills, common miseries, and common gripes might be the connecting band between some youngsters. Games of skill to be played by two or three lend themselves well to the formation of sub-groups, even a game of chess or checkers, a ping-pong game where some lonely youngsters might find a personal contact with each other which transcends the activity. Common hobbies serve as excellent media for sub-group formations. Stamp collectors, model airplane builders, and radio mechanics will by necessity spend a great deal of time with each other and get to know and need each other in the process. Then there are the "brothers in misery," the two home-sick youngsters who decide to run away together, or the three homely girls who happen to be without a date on party evenings. They do not particularly like each other but they find some con-solation in their common bitterness and frustration. Therefore, they spend a good deal of time together bemoaning their ill fate and detesting the rest of the world.

While submission to the leaders and seeking their approval is a common quality of all followers, cliques are distinguished by the amount of ambivalence and hostility against leaders. The degree of this unspoken hostility might become another criterion for clique formations. Their secret might be the unseating of the in-group. Not all followers are necessarily clique members. Some individuals in the group do not belong to any definite sub-group and are still not isolates. Their self-centeredness does not permit them to join any sub-group for long. They have no desire for deep friendships, but they do not withdraw from the group. They have group-desirable skills and interests, and can well maintain a certain independence. They are not interested and do not share in any of the cliques' secrets.

Clique formation is nothing stationary. It is frequently a rather short-lived process. Children change friendships and ties very rapidly. Suddenly one discovers that the sub-group alignment in a cottage group has changed considerably over a period of a few months, and that only a few of the same children have remained in the same sub-groups. It is interesting to speculate on the reasons why some sub-groups continue for long periods and others break up rather rapidly.

This sub-group formation, just as in-group formation and group code development, is not a conscious but rather a spontaneous, dynamic process. Children sense this process rather than under-stand it. They live it rather than plan it. However, the adult who works with the group has to understand this process and in essence to promote it in order to be fully helpful to the group.

Child-care workers have to understand the followers in order to be able to help them. They often tend to identify with the followers in their ambivalent feelings against the leaders. Often they cannot understand why a nice intelligent boy like Johnny follows a rough guy like Jack. They do not understand why Johnny gives Jack half of his birthday cake before he even tastes it himself. Quite frequently they are inclined to protect Johnny from being exploited by Jack. This protection is important when Johnny's safety or self-respect is affected, but in general this is not the case. Johnny's desire to be accepted by Jack is stronger than his need to be protected.

The child-care worker has a number of functions with the follower. He helps him to be accepted or at least tolerated by the in-group. He might help him develop and use skills which the leaders respect. The child-care worker can help the child find friends with whom he can share activities, interests and secrets within the group. He has to be aware that secrecy is a very important part of juvenile friendships, and that clique formation is an essential part of group living. True, he has to be on the alert lest these cliques develop into delinquent gangs. He can enhance the process of clique formation by placing together in bedrooms, or around the dinner table, children who have something in common and would tend to form a clique and establish a friendship group.

The child-care worker has to see that the in-group does not become too entrenched in its position. He can avoid this by distributing the members of the in-group into other groups for sleeping, eating, recreational and routine activities so that they have to be with other children and depend on them part of each day. The child-care worker has to assess each of the followers as to his potential leadership qualities. In what areas can he exert leadership? How much opportunity does he have to exert such leadership? He can sometimes gear the program so that a follower has an opportunity for leadership in some part of group life. Such opportunities arise often in games and special events during the year. Louis, who is not a leader, might be a good master of ceremonies, know a lot about dance records, or play the bugle well around a campfire. He might be an excellent runner or skater. These skills must be utilized by clever programming to raise the individual's self-confidence and his status in the group.

The child-care worker has to help each of the followers to recognize that they have a right to be themselves. He has to support them in developing enough security to express their individuality in word and action, even if it differs from the expectation of group leaders or adults.

The child-care worker should impart the feeling that he is impartial and not afraid of the leader. He must protect all the children from any misuse of leadership. The child-care worker's attitude towards group interaction between followers and leaders should be one of benevolent neutrality. He should avoid taking sides for or against the leader, except when really necessary to protect the group.

The group interactive process does not operate all the time. A great deal of the time the children are not followers or leaders but just themselves. The need for isolation from the group, for being unburdened of the responsibility either of leadership or of followership is great in all children and has to be respected. At these times a child is not an isolate but an individual seeking privacy. Sometimes child-care workers are themselves too involved in the process of group formation. They always want children to do something together and are perturbed if they seem to drift apart. Child-care workers can use these moments well to get close to individual children. The group program has to make provision for the children's need to be away from the group. This is not only important in terms of a balanced program for the individual child, but essential in terms of a balanced relationship of adults to children. If the child-care worker wants to talk to Johnny alone while the group is in the process of selecting a team for a basketball game, he will be rejected by Johnny and by the leaders of the activity. If, however, he finds another moment when no such absorbing group processes are going on Johnny may be eager to seize the opportunity for conversation.

SUMMARY

Most of the children in a living unit are followers. They often join with others to form sub-groups and cliques which are held together by common interests, skills, hostility and misery. They always share some common secrets. They follow the leader-group but have ambivalent feelings about the leaders. The child-care worker should help followers demonstrate leadership qualities in areas where they can do so. He also has to allow for a sufficient amount of privacy to all children in the group.

The Gang

Here is the problem of negative leadership within the group endangering the adult's role. The gang is a sub-group of three or four children, exclusive in membership, usually led by one ruthless domineering personality who has a magnetic appeal to other members of the gang. Physical strength, manipulative shrewdness, bragging independence of adult approval and militant defiance of authority are characteristics of the gang leader. The avowed intention of the gang leader is to usurp the power of the adult, to annihilate law and order and to establish an anti-social unity in the group. Quite frequently adults are so concerned about this form of negative leadership that they suspect every in-group of being a gang. Child-care workers must check themselves carefully so that they do not contrast the positive with the negative, the good with the bad. If there is a gang formation, the whole group cohesion and constructive group order is threatened and some definite steps must be taken. The leaders must be dethroned. The child-care worker has to face them definitely and calmly with the effect of their behavior, and have them know that he will not tolerate their attitude, that no one will be allowed to destroy the unity of the group. He has to make it clear to them that they prolong their own and other children's stay at the institution, since they make it impossible for the others to benefit from institutional facilities, that in effect this action is directed against themselves and the other children rather than against the adults. Sometimes a gang can be broken up by removal of one member. Close cooperation is necessary between child-care worker, supervisor, administration, and caseworkers in order to solve this problem. Sometimes rearrangement of bedrooms, separating gang members from each other during the night, is a help. Sometimes temporary isolation of one member into other quarters might be advisable. In institutions with several group living units the problem can sometimes be solved by transferring some of the gang members into another unit. In some extreme situations a youngster's discharge from the institution might be necessary.

It is necessary to assure the children who are terrorized by the gang that they will be protected. It is impossible for any child to be helped in an institution if he feels that the adults are not able to protect him from the other children. Just as the individual child needs protection from outside dangers and from his own impulses, the group also needs protection from gang domination within the institution. Such protection is sometimes harder to provide because there are so many ways in which gang members can terrorize individual children. Institutions have to look into their intake policy so that they do not create situations in which gang formation becomes unavoidable. In deciding on the intake of any child, one has to be aware not only of the needs of the individual child but also of the child's effect on the group. The child-care worker's observation as to potential gang formation is of great importance to the staff.

In dealing with an existing gang it is essential that the child-care worker show no fear. He must remember that these gangsters are most unhappy children who have joined together because they have lost hope. They do not like themselves and are convinced that no one likes them. They express their self-depreciation and feeling of worthlessness by banding together for mutual support. Each one is usually a desperate, frightened person, and needs a great deal of support, a feeling of worthwhileness, and a feeling that adults trust him. This major task of the child-care worker takes much patience and effort. His approval cannot be offered at the expense of the well-being and development of the other children.

The adult's fear of the group is sometimes very real. It would be self-deception to deny it. Everyone working with very disturbed individuals has experienced this at one time or another. As the child-care worker becomes aware of such fears and discusses them with his supervisor, he can recognize to what degree they interfere with his work with the group. He can see what help he needs and what measures must be taken to overcome his fear and to regain group control.

The Isolate

The child who belongs neither to the in-group nor to any sub-group is an isolate. He is lonely, does not have the sense of belonging and feels unwanted. The movement of the isolate into the group and the speed at which this movement proceeds is actually the major measuring rod for the success of the group living process. Constant absorption of isolates into the group is necessary in order to make institutional treatment an important and constructive experience for them. While every child feels at times alone and isolated, the isolates' status of separateness from the group process is a consistent one. They are forced into that state by inner or outer forces, and cannot leave it at will and join the group.

There are three major types of isolates: the stranger in the group; the withdrawn child; and the group-rejected child (the outcast). Any child upon first entering the group is for a period of time an isolate. This period might last only an hour, or it might last several weeks. If the new child already knows someone in the group before he comes, if he has many of the essential group qualities and skills, if he has a good judgment of the group values and constellation, and if he has an outgoing personality ready and eager to move towards the group right from the beginning, his period of isolation might be very short. However, most new children need some time before they become a part of the group. The new child usually does not know who is who in the group, who the leaders are, in what cliques the followers are sub-divided, and what the group code is. He needs time to find his way into the group. The group itself is often threatened by the arrival of a newcomer. They feel that their security and group status might be affected by the new arrival. They are suspicious of him. They wonder how he will fit in, and usually look at him with caution and guardedness. This does not obviate the fact that they often are friendly and hospitable to him. They may even give him a welcome party, offer to show him around the institution, or take him along to recreational activities. They usually remember their own arrival and the period of isolation they had experienced. They comply quite often with the request of adults to make the newcomer feel at home. Anxiety and hostility toward the newcomer often underlies this facade of hospitality.

A group of adolescents may have a welcome party for the new child and act friendly with him. Then at night after the adults retire they might subject him to an "initiation" whereby they strip his bed, turn his mattress over, and impose a number of tortures upon him demonstrating their hostile feelings. It seems that the more defensive and anxious the newcomer is, the more hostile and sadistic becomes the behavior of the group. Frequently other isolates are more hospitable to the newcomer. Very often group-rejected children will seek a way into the group through the newcomer. They become the newcomer's guide for a day or two. They are quite obtrusive at times in their eagerness to make him feel at home, and then after a few days, when the newcomer is not a stranger any more and is in the process of being accepted by the group, they feel deserted and more painfully aware of their isolation from the group. Sometimes a clique accepts the newcomer readily in the hope this will strengthen them, especially if there are rival cliques within the group.

The child-care worker can shorten this period of isolation for the stranger in the group. The first step must be taken before the child's entry into the group. He has to prepare the group for the child. He has to give them some knowledge about the child, his assets and skills, and his obvious shortcomings. If he knows the child is a good chess player or an expert mechanic, he should let the group know about it. In order to be able to do this the child-care worker must get adequate information himself. The supervisor and/or the caseworker should see that the child-care worker gets sufficient information before the child comes (see Chapter 2), so that he himself can better understand the new child, and can help the group understand him. With the group he should "accentuate the positive" traits of the child without withholding negative features that are obvious anyway. He must, however, not share the child's past history with the group. Such sharing would violate the code of professional confidentiality.

In the first days of the newcomer's stay at the institution the child-care worker has to be available to him. He must explain to him the routines and the manner of living in the unit, so that the newcomer knows such things as who is on duty, and where to go for his allowance, and clothing. He must know who will give him permission to leave the living unit; who makes arrangements for school and what are his duties in the group. Very important is the assignment of the child to a bedroom and a seat at the dining room table. The newcomer needs encouragement to participate in group activities. The child-care worker can give the new child certain hints as to what the group is interested in, what the children like to do, what they like to eat. Without revealing his own preference he can indicate whom the children listen to within the group. In a positive way he can explain the qualities of each child, that Johnny is good in basketball and Jay in drawing, that Jerry knows history so well that he should appear on a quiz program. From the very beginning he can help the child see the positives in other children. However, he should not give a child any direct advice as to which children in the group he should choose as friends. The new child has to assess this for himself. The child-care worker can give him an idea of what the group code is. He can say something like, "In this cottage they don't like anybody who snitches," or, "In this cottage they loan clothes to each other, but they don't like children to take the clothes without asking." This has to be done discreetly so that the newcomer does not feel pushed into the group, but rather feels the adult's help in his own search for group acceptance.

The second type of isolate is separated from the group mainly because of his personality. Some psychological forces within compel him to withdraw. Fear of the group, suspicion, insecurity, and an overwhelming preoccupation with himself make it impossible for him to participate in group life. The painful experiences he has had prior to coming to the institution show themselves in this type of child in complete withdrawal. The withdrawn child usually has a poor assessment of reality and a limited capacity to comply and succeed in it. His ego is so loaded down by his own feelings that it cannot extend or invest itself in any other people in his surroundings. Somewhere in his past he has been hurt by people socially and psychologically to such a degree that he does not dare relate to people again. In some cases he feels guilty about something he did or thought he did, to others or to himself. These feelings are so great that he fears he is not worthy of social recognition by others. He feels different from others, socially handicapped and mutilated. Other withdrawn children are so convinced that the whole world is against them that anything one does is interpreted as an act of persecution or as an attack. They are so convinced that everybody wants to pick on them, that they will always find reasons in other people's behavior which they can interpret as persecution.

At a party in one of the cottages the children had paper napkins in red, white and blue, and had placed them in this order on the table. Jane, a very withdrawn, suspicious girl, happened to get a seat with a red napkin. She was very upset about it and suspected that people thought she was a Communist and marked her by giving her a red napkin. Some weeks later when somebody wanted to give her a yellow scarf she reacted with the same vehemence against this, which she interpreted as meaning she was a coward.

However, the suspicion is usually not so obvious. It is somewhat more hidden and children do not express it so directly. Sometimes, in order to hide their fears and insecurity, these withdrawn children shroud themselves in arrogance. They say they will not come to a party because it's "kid stuff." They would not participate in a game because "nobody plays it right anyway." Sometimes withdrawn children express their insecurity and fears more openly; they admit they are afraid. They admit they can not dance. They cry readily. They get panicky easily and do not show the strength of self-control that most children in the group show. They do not even attempt to show a veneer of strength and respectability. For instance, during a thunderstorm they might hide their heads in the pillows, or they might show extreme fears about getting sick.

Many of these fears are present in the other children too, but are better hidden and controlled.

The withdrawn child presents a problem to other children in the group. They are confused rather than threatened by him. They are exhausted by his behavior rather than annoyed. At times they are amused rather than antagonized by it. When their first attempts to include him in the group fail, they somehow give up. They know that Johnny is not a good sport. They also sense that he is very unhappy. They are, of course, most annoyed by the type of withdrawn child who appears arrogant and stuckup, and they might at times take rather sadistic pleasure in throwing him out. On the other hand they feel a deep sympathy for the child who is admittedly unhappy and helpless. The group code in the adolescent groups usually protects and forbids the torture of such a child. The leaders protect him once they recognize his helplessness. Children recognize the social difficulties of the withdrawn child, and they label him "queer," a "character," a "sissy," or just plain "nuts." These characterizations usually do not imply much hostility.

The child-care worker can play a very important role with the withdrawn child. He can become the bridge between the child and the group. He must be aware that this child is basically afraid of the group and cannot be forced into the group prematurely. Any method of accelerating his entry into the group has to be used very carefully and with great sensitivity. In contrast to followers, the withdrawn boy or girl usually has a greater need to be accepted by adults. He is in dire need of protection. His only companionship for the time being comes from the adult. The adult should make himself available as much as possible to this child in order to give him some opportunity to communicate with people. Sometimes the child-care worker tries to move this child too quickly into the group. Often, instead of giving him outlets in which he can find satisfactions by himself, such as books, games, craft activities or a small radio set, which would all enable him to find some peace within himself before he moves into the group, the child-care worker is inclined to minimize and actually deny the need for such private activity. Sometimes the child-care worker even derides the child for this need in order to make him move into the group.

Such a premature "pushing" in the direction of group participation very often has the reverse effect.

The opposite attitude on the part of the adult is much more desirable; namely, that it is perfectly all right to be alone, to play by oneself, or to read; that it is no tragedy not to participate in games. The child-care worker might draw the withdrawn youngster into a discussion. Sometimes he might play a game of chess or checkers with him. Perhaps after a while he can choose a game in which a third person can participate, like Chinese Checkers. If the child-care worker can see that this youngster is not exposed to cruelty by the group, it gives the group some direction in understanding such peculiar behavior, and he can create an atmosphere of tolerance for the withdrawn child. Yet the child-care worker should not over-protect the child from the group or excuse him from all participation in group functions, like bedtime, meals, and certain chores. However, he can help him to carry out such functions.

Richard, a very withdrawn and somewhat awkward boy of twelve, had so much trouble participating in any household chores that he at times detained the whole group by his ineptitude. When he had the chore of clearing the table after the meal, he broke so many dishes that he had to be assigned to another job, in which he did not function much better. Finally, the child-care worker allowed him to be free of any chores. The group, which had good-naturedly tolerated Richard's difficulties, became quite angry at this "privilege," and called him lazy. Some of them decided to imitate his ineptitude by dropping dishes deliberately. Richard, who used the time when other children did their chores to withdraw even more than before, told his caseworker that the child-care worker's relieving him of household responsibilities was a "sure proof" that he was "crazy." After a while, the child-care worker assigned him to the chore of helping her fold sheets and laundry.

The peculiar behavior of the withdrawn child has to be interpreted to the other children over and over in simple, matter-of-fact terms, so that they can tolerate the special attention that has to be given to this youngster.

The most difficult type of isolate for the child-care worker is the group-rejected child. The new child will sooner or later become a member of the group. The withdrawn child usually can win the group's tolerance and patience. However, the group-rejected isolate somehow antagonizes the group so much that he is a constant object of attack, ridicule, discrimination, and exclusion. The group does not extend to him the tolerance granted the withdrawn child. He is the scapegoat of the group. He is openly rejected and is knocked around, pushed, and insulted, so that he is constantly physically and emotionally hurt. He is an outcast, a child that nobody wants; nobody wants him in his bedroom, in activities, or even to be seen with him. Such a child constantly comes to the child-care worker for protection until he finally exasperates the adult too because of this constant need.

What is the matter with the outcast? All children who want to be members of the group need to have certain qualifications. They have to assess realistically the powers in the group. They have to assess realistically the rules of the group—the group code. The outcast does not know the powers in the group. He does not attempt to feel his way into the group in order to understand them. Rather than to wait, he pretends that he knows it all. He rushes headlong into the group. He denies his helplessness. He goes into a counter-attack against the group and the group code without realistic regard for the group's power. He is so preoccupied with himself that he cannot look objectively at anyone else. Usually he does not have many group-desirable skills and interests. He combines this lack of reality awareness and lack of ability with a tremendous aggressiveness against the group which he cannot control. He immediately takes offense, and cannot wait. He tries to enter the group by means unacceptable to them.

> Louis came into a cottage where playing baseball was a favorite group activity. He remarked that baseball players are "idiots," that he would not get his hands dirty with a baseball. He added boastingly that he would not play the game. He could quote Latin poetry, and, of course, knowledge of Latin poetry was not at all a desirable skill. The group immediately picked up on this and identified the boy as "Nero."

This youngster used arrogance and counterattack as defense mechanisms. He verbally attacked the leaders in a totally hopeless battle in which he had to come out the loser. He provoked the group against him and failed to follow up his bravado with deeds. He minimized the group's achievements, derided their skills and values, and thus got himself involved in a self punishing process where he always ended up the victim.

The group-rejected child really wants to be a member of the group at all costs, but he does not want to be a follower. He would like to be a leader right away, and in his clumsy way tries to unseat the leaders. He can see himself only as an unique individualist, never as an equal. He is not secure enough to be a follower. He sees himself either as excluded from the group in splendid isolation or on top of the group as the illustrious leader. Since he fails in the latter goal he assumes the former. Not only does he not have group-acceptable skills and interests, but he does not have courage either. Indeed, he is afraid. Yet instead of admitting his fear of the group he tries in his infantile way to keep them in fear of himself. He does this by informing on the children, by constantly asking for the adult's protection, by carrying tales from one child to the other, by instigating discord between the children, by disturbing their fun, and by other such methods.

The group very soon not only recognizes the "phoniness" of the child's defenses, but also the fear behind his boisterous manner. They also recognize how easy it is really to break down his defenses, so they tease and bait him to show up his cowardice. He represents to them everything they do not want to be. In a way he expresses for them their worst image of themselves. Often the group's attitude is an important gauge in the diagnosis of these children. Sometimes the child who is group-rejected over a long period of time actually cannot be treated at the institution. The group's diagnosis can at times be more accurate than that of the intake workers who admitted the child. While diagnosis of the outcast by the group as "queer" and "nuts" is loaded with hostility and rejection, it is significant and should not be ignored. It may be a sign of the sickness of the outcast as well as of the relatively healthy reaction of the group.

There is no doubt that next to the gang leader, the group-rejected child is the most serious problem for the child-care worker. He has the constant job of protection because this child is often in direct danger of being physically or emotionally abused by the other children. On the other hand this protection can have a negative effect. The more the child-care worker protects him the more rejected the outcast will be by the group. Furthermore, the child care worker might jeopardize his own status with the group by protecting the outcast, because the group extends the hostility against the outcast to his protectors. Thus the interaction between outcast, group and child-care worker can easily develop into a vicious circle. Nevertheless the outcast has to be protected. The difficult question is how the child-care worker can protect the outcast from all the other children. The child-care worker must know where his own limitations lie. He has to be quite frank with both the group and the group-rejected child as to what behavior he can tolerate. He has to show the group that he understands their anger towards the outcast, but that he cannot allow them to hurt any child. He has to be ready to admit to the outcast that while he can protect him in many cases, he cannot protect him in all. He can show him how he antagonizes and provokes the group, and perhaps try to encourage him to be more withdrawn and less aggressive. Sometimes the only achievable goal for the child-care worker is to isolate the child, to give him something to do that will keep him away from the group; to admit to him that he is not yet liked by the other children and to encourage him to stay away from them and carry his loneliness a little more bravely. At the same time he must try to give him hope that he will ultimately be accepted by the group. The child-care worker has to work closely with this child's caseworker or therapist. Contact with adults outside the group living unit is advisable for the outcast. Time might be set aside when this child can be with someone, perhaps a maintenance worker, a secretary, the librarian, the chaplain, or some volunteer, who is tolerant of his behavior and at the same time can keep him occupied in enjoyable activity.

The child-care worker has to work with the group about its attitude toward this child. He has to assure the group again and again that this child's behavior is not deliberate but rather that he cannot help it. He may indicate how the group's reaction against him prohibits instead of promoting his improvement. At the same time he has to let the group see that he understands their negative reactions toward the youngster and that in protecting him he is not rejecting the rest of the group. If after a few months the child-care worker cannot break down the wall of rejection which surrounds the outcast he has to raise the question with the proper authority as to whether this child should remain in the group or move into another, less rejecting group. Isolation during some especially difficult periods of the day, such as single room sleeping arrangements, may be tried to alleviate the situation long enough for the child to become more secure and to work out with his therapist some of the problems leading to his being rejected. It is important always to remember that a tremendous amount of patience, tolerance, understanding, sympathy and time is needed to help such a child. He is unhappy, terribly fearful, and suspicious, but cannot admit these feelings. In a way one has to react to him by consciously increasing his isolation from the group, more than he himself wants it. It may be necessary to neutralize the group reaction toward him by giving him outlets in which he can succeed outside the group and by being near him as much as possible while he is in the group.

SUMMARY

The most specific contribution an institution makes to the education and treatment of a child is the group living process. This process is based on the interaction of the children with each other, and with the adults in charge of the living unit. The proper balance between group participation and privacy is essential for the healthy development of the child in the group, and the program of the group must provide such a balance. The regularity and community of experiences links children together in spite of differences and discrepancies in their individual background and personalities. While many group activities must necessarily be compulsory, there are many opportunities for voluntary group activities within an institutional group which can be utilized by the child-care worker. In order to be effective with the group the child-care worker has to understand the group constellation and group code. The first is the interaction between leaders (in-group), followers, and isolates within the group. This interaction and the constant flow from the state of isolation toward the in-group makes the group living process a dynamic and therapeutic experience. The latter is the set of rules the group sets up for itself, unwritten and unspoken, but nevertheless well known and observed by its members.

CHAPTER 3

Meals and the Meaning of Food

When the children are washed, dressed, and ready for breakfast, breakfast should be ready for them. We will discuss at this time all the meals and their importance.

Food has four main values for every human being. (1.) It has nutritional value, and as such is one of the prime necessities of life. (2.) It has an enjoyment value and is one of the basic pleasures of life. An extraordinary amount of energy, effort, and thinking goes into making food enjoyable as well as nutritional. One of the major distinctions between the human being and the animal is emphasis on the palatability of food. (3.)It has psychological value. From early infancy, food has more than just a nutritional and pleasurable effect. Actually, the process of eating, the experience of being fed by an adult, and the attitude toward food all have great impact on the development of the child's personality and his attitude toward life. (4.) It has a social value. The regularity as well as the sociability of eating in any group of people, be it the family, a Boy Scout troop, a company of soldiers, a crew of factory workers, or the members of an exclusive club, form personality ties between the participants. When adults remember childhood, their most pleasant memories often center around the family gathering at a dinner table. Family cohesiveness can often be evaluated by the number of meals they have together, and the spirit of this to-getherness.

In an institution these major values, nutritional, pleasure, social and psychological, must be considered in planning and serving food. One of these values without others will not suffice. Food that is good for the blood and bones must also be good for the palate. Meals offer outstanding group-forming opportunities. If these opportunities are not utilized, institutions do not use group living in its fullest potentials.

Nutritional Value of Food

Most institutional diets meet the basic nutritional requirements set up by medical and dietary experts. The balance of proteins, carbohydrates, fats, minerals, the importance of well cooked, adequate quantities of food, the use of vegetables, meats, fish, grain, dairy products, fruits, sugar, salt, and water, the adjustment of the diet in accordance with the age group and special dietary needs of individual children (for instance, the under-nourished child or the obese child) have become uncontested tenets in our society. Fortunately the economy of our country permits us to abide by these tenets and to offer a healthy diet in almost all institutions. It is imperative that sound nutritional views on quantity and kind of food are observed in an institution, and that someone on the institutional staff has the expertness and authority to see that basic nutritional requirements are met. If a dietician is a member of the institutional staff she should regularly discuss meal planning with the administration and the staff pediatrician. If the person in charge of food planning is not a trained dietician this is even more necessary. Usually, therefore, the child-care worker needs to be relatively little concerned with the basic nutritional values of the food in the institution. There may be exceptions. In some institutions these requirements may not be satisfactorily supplied. Only in these few instances must the child-care worker deal with the nutritional value of food. If he is convinced that the nutritional requirements are not fulfilled, he should inform the dietician. Some knowledge of these factors is desirable for any child-care worker. If the institutional menu is based on an inadequate diet, this should be corrected. It is necessary sometimes to explain the nutritional values to the children, and to interpret to them why certain foods appear on the menu, although they do not particularly like them. The child-care worker not only can help the children understand the need for certain foods but also he can show them the institution's interest in their healthy and normal growth. Some children in institutions may come from cultures where vegetables were rejected, and meat and milk were the major part of the menu. The child-care worker who assists this child slowly to change his dietary patterns to include vegetables and other basic foods helps him in his growth and adjustment.

Pleasure Value of Food

Aside from a few exceptional cases there need not be any conflict between the nutritional and pleasure value of food. Indeed in practice the nutritional value of food depends on the pleasure value. No matter how healthy certain foods might be, if the children do not like them they will not eat them. Less nutritional foods might in practice have more nutritional value because the children eat them. The proof of the pudding is in the eating. There is almost no basic food item that can only be given in one particular form. Meats, vegetables, and dairy products can be prepared in many ways. One of these many forms is usually palatable to a child. The child who doesn't like milk might like ice cream. The child who doesn't like spinach might like broccoli, cauliflower, or perhaps asparagus. The child who doesn't like cooked vegetables might like raw vegetables or salads. The child who doesn't like stewed prunes might like uncooked prunes. Financial considerations exclude certain food items, but even within one price range there is usually enough variety possible with imagination, good planning, and an interest in the preparation of food. The areas of pleasure and satisfaction for most institutional children are considerably more limited than of other children. They often do not like their social status, friends, families, peers, and schools. Food is usually one source of pleasure. Pleasure is necessary to healthy growth. For deprived children, it also has therapeutic meaning.

Everything must therefore be done to make the meals pleasant. Human beings have different tastes. Foods which one person likes are detested by others. In every family there is a certain amount of conflict about individual taste patterns. Sometimes mothers or fathers superimpose their own taste patterns on the rest of the family. Sometimes the child's taste patterns determine the family menu. Usually certain concessions are made to each member, compromises are reached, so that over a period of time every member of the family feels that his food tastes are sufficiently met. Families, of course, have a great advantage since children take on their parents' taste patterns during the many years of family living, and taste discrepancies in the family are lessened.

In an institution where children come from many different families, taste patterns vary widely. Every institutional child-care worker should ask himself what the taste pattern of each child is. For instance, if he had to order a menu for Johnny alone, what would it be? Such a question serves not only as a guide for possible suggestions to the institution's kitchen, but also as a self-test of his knowledge of the individual child. What kind of food does each child like best? How do the individual child's food patterns compare with his nutritional needs, with the food patterns of other children, and with the existing institutional menu? Child-care workers need not worry about discrepancies between the children's food patterns and nutritional values. Even if they prefer certain foods, children usually balance their own diet sufficiently in the long run. Having experienced for a time the pleasure of eating, they will develop a more tolerant attitude to all kinds of food, even those that they do not particularly like.

How do these individual preferences relate to each other? How can the nine children in a group, or the fifty children in an institution, enjoy the same food if individual tastes vary so much? In order to answer this question one must first find out what the differences are. Often an institution does not even try to find out what individual preferences are. Usually the differences are not so great as it seems. Often children differ more about the way a certain dish is prepared than about the food item itself. A compromise can easily be reached by discussing it with the group. Such a discussion can become a factor in the socialization of the children. How does one overcome the conflict between the individual and group preferences on one hand, and the budgetary limitations on the other? What happens when the children want strawberry short-cake or steak every day? This can be discussed and made part of their socialization process. If the children know what the limitations are they can better adjust to them and make compromises. Yet the first guide for an institutional diet ought to be the children themselves, their own palates. A food that is wasted or rejected is the most expensive one in the long run. While this formula is admittedly an over-simplification, it still presents the most realistic device for institutional food planning.

Good food planning must be matched by good cooking. Even the best planned meal can be spoiled by an inadequate cook. Institutional food should not only be attractive and palatable, but—if at all possible—should also avoid the feeling of mass production and retain as much as possible the individual touch.

The way in which food is served is an important factor. Food should be attractive not only to the taste but also to the eye and the nose. The way in which food is placed before the children is often an inducing or deterring factor to their appetite. Even children who like ice cream do not eat it if it is half melted, and those who like soup might reject it if it is cold when served. Sometimes institutional equipment is not adequate to serve the food attractively. For instance, in some institutions children have toast for breakfast. There must be sufficient toasters available and the toast must be warm when served. Modern kitchen equipment permits that food even in greater quantities can be served in an adequate and individualized way. Modern restaurants have solved most of these difficulties, and there is no reason why institutions cannot. It is important for the child-care worker to observe what specific taste problems arise around the preparation and serving of food in order to adjust equipment and methods to the needs of the group. How many servings should a child be allowed? Should he have one, two, or three? This depends on the child's appetite, and the amount of food available. There must be enough food available for the individual child's eating patterns, even if this means temporary waste of food.

Food Fads and Special Diets

Some children have food fads and phobias that make it impossible
for them to eat certain foods. They can overcome these phobias
and fads only with support and treatment. This takes time. Rigid
insistence that the children partake of disliked food makes the
meal torture for them rather than a pleasure. Most children can
be encouraged to try some of everything. This too must be done
with flexibility and understanding. Special patience is necessary
with the child suffering from food phobias. Just as a sick child
must live on a diet, children with food fads cannot be expected to
eat the foods that they have abhorred most of their lives. Slowly,
as they see that the child-care worker understands them, they will
be able to try some of the food that they detested in the past. It is
the goal of all educators and parents to teach the children to eat
as many different foods as possible. The method used to obtain this
goal must be one of sympathy with their food fads and patience
rather than rigidity, regimentation, or ridicule.

Children who, because of their physical conditions, must live on
a special diet present serious problems. This should be discussed
with the supervisor and if necessary with the pediatrician who
ordered the diet. Obese or under-nourished children cannot be
pushed rapidly into following a diet. Sometimes one loses more
than one gains by forcing a regimen on them for which they are
not ready. The obese girl who should reduce, but likes fattening
food, will not be helped if she is told that she is unattractive and
will never get a boy friend. She already knows this and is worried
about it. She is also worried about her lack of will power to change
herself. She might be pushed into defiance. She might deny any
interest in boys, and go on demonstrating her independence by
overeating even more. She must first be convinced that the child-
care worker wants her to have a good time and wants her to eat.
She must first be sure that people accept her as she is, not only as
they think she ought to be. When a reducing diet is recommended
for a child it is important that the adult lets him feel that he wants
him to enjoy his meals, that the restriction is not an act of rejection but rather one of assistance and interest. A cottage mother

who worked with an obese child stated, "I bribe her into a diet," meaning that she buys her extra clothing, gives her extra help with her hair, and shows in many ways a special interest in her in order to help her restrict her food intake.

Where the diet is necessary because of an acute physical illness, such as diabetes or intestinal disorders, the medical requirements must be the first consideration. Control of such a diet is imperative. A good deal of interpretation must be given to such a child in order to help him understand that this is something which is done for him rather than against him. It is particularly important to see to it that the diet is as varied and tasteful as possible.

Psychological Value of Food

In addition to its nutritional value and its pleasure to the palate, food has a very important psychological value. There are several aspects to this. First, the process itself of eating, using lips and mouth, represents an important human satisfaction and security. Psychologists have, for instance, found that in the small baby the process of sucking is almost as important as that of eating, and that infants who do not do enough sucking in their first year of life— even though they have enough food—develop undesirable personality traits which may stay with them throughout their lives. The most important aspect for our discussion is the child's relationship to the adult which develops in respect to food, and the meaning of this relationship in the child's personality development. For a child, all food intake necessitates the participation of at least two people, the child himself who eats and the one who gives food, in the normal family, usually the mother. The value of food for the child is greatly determined by the adult's attitude, the attention, affection, patience, warmth, and readiness with which he or she gives food. Mothers, while nursing, always hold their babies close, transmitting warmth and togetherness along with nutrition. Pediatricians today are as much concerned with the emotional ingredients of the feeding process as with the nutritional values.

What is true for the infant is true for the growing child. The attitude with which food is given, whether by the mother or a mother substitute, is important. The child needs to feel that the adult enjoys feeding him, that every piece of food symbolizes a "piece of love." The child-care worker has to be aware of this. Small children dawdle over meals. The help an adult can give them by sitting with them, coaxing them, encouraging them and even if necessary feeding them is part of the mothering they need. With all children the personal interest the adult takes in their food, in increasing the pleasure, the strength, and the growth they derive from it, is as essential for their emotional growth as is the physical value. Actually the very same food tastes better to children if it is served or prepared by a person they particularly like and whose interest and affection they are sure of. Most children in institutions compare the institutional food unfavorably with their mother's cooking, even in cases where the mother was a notably poor cook. It is not really the cooking but the mothering they miss.

> In a cottage of twelve-year-old boys, the children refused to eat any soup prepared by the cook, who was a rather stern and unapproachable woman. When the cook became ill the well liked cottage mother prepared a soup for them according to the recipe given to her by the cook. The children not only ate the soup, but insisted, on the return of the cook, that she use the cottage mother's recipe in the future.

Another aspect of the psychological value of food is the security the child receives through food intake. The infant who cries when he is hungry and finds each time that his mother comes to feed him, finally does not have to cry any more—he can wait. He is sure that the mother will come and he will be fed. Even if after a while he has to wait a few minutes for the food he will be able to do so without deep distress. He has learned to wait or, to say it in a different way, he had enough security to develop self-control or "ego." The child, however, who cried in vain for his mother, who was not fed regularly, who could not rely on the adult does not develop this basic security. He will continue to yell impatiently for his food in one way or another. Even as an adult he may not have developed patience and self-control. Many children in institutions have experienced in their early years a lack of security in relation to food. Some have experienced deprivation. The child-care worker should know this background of frustration in order to understand the children's attitude toward food—and to help them with it.

In some cases it was less deprivation than an adult's inconsistency which left its mark on the child. A mother might have appeased the child with any food he liked when he yelled loud enough and have practically forgotten to feed him when he did not yell, or she might have overfed him one day and underfed him the next. Often, such early experiences are not known to the child-care worker and the professional staff. The mother frequently does not report them to the caseworker; indeed, she may have forgotten them altogether. Very often the child's emotional attitude to food is a clue to what his early life might have been like. The child-care worker's observations can greatly help the professional staff to understand better not only the child's present but also possibly his past experiences.

Frequently one observes a child who gobbles down his food as though someone was waiting to take it away from him. It would be interesting to speculate (even better to find out) whether he had been given enough time to eat when he was an infant. A busy mother might withdraw her breast or the bottle when the baby was still hungry. Then there is the child who eagerly heaps a pile of food on his plate, which he can never consume. He keeps his plate filled, yet when the meal is over he has not eaten it all, thus wasting food. Perhaps previously he has had to compete with older brothers who cleaned up the platters so rapidly that there was never a second helping left for him, and he had to make sure that he would get all he possibly could eat in his first helping.

Some children need the security of knowing that they can have all the food they want and that no one will take it away from them. After a while the child-care worker can usually convince them that there will always be enough and that, if they want another serving, they can certainly have it. The child-care worker might even reserve on the platter part of the food for their second serving, and show them this "reserved" portion, which they may have after they have finished their first. This assurance will give them the chance to take smaller portions at first and wait for seconds. Other children may have too little food on their plates. They become upset if they get more than they can eat. Sometimes in these cases the children had been forced by their mothers to eat food they did not want, and were threatened because they refused to eat. These children should be permitted to take a minimum of food, even though the child-care worker might have some doubts as to whether they are eating enough for sustenance. After ɑ while such a child is convinced that he will never be forced at the institution to eat more than he wants and will probably slowly increase his food intake.

Children who have experienced deprivation react in many different ways. Some hoard food. Suddenly a child-care worker discovers a slice of bread, a piece of cake, or an apple hidden under a youngster's pillow or in his locker, and wonders why the child, who can have these items any time, should hide them like stolen treasure.

There is the dawdler, who takes an unduly long time; perhaps his mother could not set any limits and allowed him all the time he wanted for eating. He might have used this to control his mother and keep her away from anybody else as long as possible. There is the child with food fads, the overeater, the undereater, the fellow who checks everyone else's plate jealously to see that nobody gets a better deal, the griper who cannot find anything good about any of the food, the enthusiast who seems to fall in love with every piece of food, the youngster who seems to think only of food, who immediately after lunch starts to talk about dinner, and the child who never gets hungry and always has to be reminded about mealtimes. All these reactions are caused by previous experience with food and food providers.

The child-care worker cannot undo in a short time attitudes which have been built up over the years. But he can give every child the feeling that he wants to feed him, to be close to him while he eats, wants to give him the best food possible and enough of it, and enough time to eat it. At the same time he can help each child feel that he is part of the group, that food, time and attention have to be given to all the children, and that eating is not only a psychological and physiological, but also a social process. There are some children who heap food on their plates at the expense of others, and there are certain food items like meats or desserts of which only a certain amount is available. Limits must be set so that each child gets his due share. Eating habits often express inner feelings. A child might show anger and hostility against the child-care worker or against his own parents by eating habits which are offensive to adults. Eating might alleviate anxiety in some children and represent one of the few areas of security and gratification.

Social Value of Food

We feel sorry for the lonely person who eats by himself. We feel slightly embarrassed when we go to a restaurant alone and see other people eating together. In even the most primitive societies, eating is a social experience. Social class, religious beliefs, age, and kinship all become criteria determining the group and the order in which one takes one's meals. The selection of food, the preparation of the table, the seating order, the timing of the meal have been organized around social values. The more refined the social group, the more important become these values. The satisfaction of hunger alone, which doubtlessly is the primary reason for any food intake, has become an almost unnoticeable part of food satisfaction, and is well covered by a system of social values. Many social groups object to people eating without observing some of the social niceties. Religious rituals based on food intake have added spiritual content to the social values.

In an institution where groups of children eat together, these social values cannot be so highly developed as in adult society, or in a well developed family setting where adults dominate the social group. Like all other socialization processes, socially organized food intake means a purposeful delay of the immediate instinct gratification in order to achieve ultimately a longer lasting, deeper, and more secure satisfaction—the feeling of being able to comply with the rules and moods of the group. The child who can wait for his dessert until the rest of the family has eaten the rest of the meal, learns not only to wait and control his drives, but also to submit his own desires to the will of the group. Only after he had many times had the reassuring experience that, after each time he waited for dessert, it was served to all, is he able to submit to the social rule.

Children who did not receive such assurance do not have the incentive or the strength to wait. They have not developed the ability to control their instinctual needs long enough to adjust to social patterns, and develop the strength for the socialization expected from them. Therefore, the social process of eating, waiting for one another, eating in a certain manner, and the order of food intake, often make greater demands on them than they can fulfill.

The child-care worker must give the children the feeling that sufficient food is available, and that the adults enjoy giving it to them. Only after they have this assurance can the process of socialization start. Table manners and socially acceptable forms of food intake must be flexible enough so a new child who deviates from them is not rejected and does not feel that observance of manners and forms are more important to the child-care worker than giving food.

Joint Menu Planning

Social forms and social participation are important. The child must become aware of the importance of the social values of food. This can be started in a children's institution before food is served. It can start with the establishment of the menu. There is no reason why children in an institution should not participate in menu planning. While the younger groups have a very limited awareness of menus, the older children take a great deal of interest in food planning. The child-care worker can show them that their own differences in food tastes make planning necessary, even if all these tastes could be satisfied. If some children like spinach, others cauliflower, some like ground meat, others chicken, they can be made to see for themselves that not all of them can get their favorite food at the same time. It is sometimes helpful to have the children plan a menu of their own. One can ask the older children to include nutritional and budgetary considerations in this menu.

Child-care workers and dieticians who have tried this are astonished at the similarity between the children's requested menus and the institutional menus. There are some differences. There are some special requests—a different kind of dessert, change in vegetables, or sometimes more seasoning in the meat. Often these requests can easily be fulfilled without additional expense or loss of nutritional value. Sometimes additional expenses would be incurred by accepting the children's suggestions. It is possible to discuss this frankly with the children. A compromise can often be reached in the form of an occasional special treat. The child-care worker can use the group to discuss the meaning of an unreasonable request with the children and can help them to recognize the reality limitations within which they have to operate. Sometimes the child-care worker may have to acknowledge with them the sad reality that the institution is not their own home and sympathize with their food requests, although they cannot be met.

The participation in menu planning has an additional purpose; it gives the children a feeling of having some influence on their environment and not being only the powerless pawns of a system of administrative and dietary regulations.

The child-care worker knows which food is eaten most frequently and which is left over. He can use the children's criticism of food to make suggestions for future menus. He can bring the children's requests to the dietician. He may have the children form a food committee to discuss it with the dietician. The child-care worker, in discussing food with the children, has to do this without hostility against the children or the administration. Sometimes child-care workers use the children's criticism to express their own criticism of the food, or on the other hand suppress their criticism totally, and defend the quality of food. A tolerant attitude is most advisable. The child-care worker can indicate that the institution wants to get the best possible food and accept the children's constructive criticism and suggestions. Group participation in food planning can be relatively easily developed. Many a group council in a children's institution started with children's complaints about food.

Participation in Food Preparation

As meal-planning can be used for socialization of the children, so can the preparing of food. This is most easily done if the living unit includes the kitchen. Even if there is no individual dining room there should be a small kitchenette in which occasional meals can be prepared. Some institutional cottages have regular kitchens in which all meals are prepared. In others only breakfast and snacks are prepared in the individual kitchen, while other meals are prepared elsewhere. Unit facilities are very useful when a group decides that they want to prepare a special meal by themselves. Baking a cake, preparing refreshments for a party, and even cooking a full meal on a special occasion are desirable activities in each living unit. Even if the kitchen facilities are centralized a child-care worker can enrich the children's lives by occasionally taking them on a cooking expedition into the central kitchen. In this way some isolates can be engaged in enjoyable group activity. The cookies which Mildred made for the group could become the key that opens the group to her. Even if the children do not themselves participate in the preparation of food, their observation of the adult working for them in the kitchen has a constructive, gratifying and socializing effect. Younger children, especially, who did not have enough mothering in their own homes need such experiences. In a normal family the child spends a good deal of time with his mother in the kitchen as her "little helper" and develops a feeling of security, warmth and belonging through these experiences. While institutions cannot replace the home atmosphere and while the kitchens may be separated from the living quarters, even institutions cannot afford to move kitchens out of the home altogether.

Meals

Breakfast, as has already been mentioned, does not usually lend itself to a formal group meal arrangement. The early morning period does not provide the appealing atmosphere for social experiences in the larger group. Institutions with individual dining rooms in each unit can easily arrange for individualized breakfast. Institutions with a central dining room might make it possible for breakfast to be eaten in the individual units. Even if such arrangements cannot be made the breakfast period could be long enough and planned so that children can have their breakfasts individually within this period.

On weekdays many children are at school for lunch, and have only a short lunch period. Some of them do not come back for lunch at all, and others have lunch at the institution, but have to hurry back to school immediately after the meal. On weekdays, therefore, lunch does not lend itself well to becoming a formal group meal. However, the order, enjoyment, and to a certain degree the formality of the main meal are requirements as necessary for the noon meal as for the evening meal. Therefore, many of the suggestions for dinner are valid for lunch, if it is a group meal at the institution.

Many children take packed lunches to school. The packing of lunches by the child-care worker can be a real demonstration of his interest in the child. The choice of the food according to the individual taste of the children, the combination of nutritional food and delectable desserts, the addition, perhaps, of a "surprise" for the child, a candy bar or a cookie, the attractiveness of the package and expectancy created by the wrapping paper, can all serve to increase the child's appreciation of his lunch, and in the long run of the people who pack it. The packed lunch of the child from the institution should neither distinguish him in quality nor appearance from the other children in the school.

In an institution, at least one meal a day should be taken in a relaxed and organized group. The evening meal lends itself very well to a group setting, and should be arranged for this purpose. Dinner should be a dignified meal, a meal for which the tables are set with tablecloths, or other attractive coverings. The children should be dressed properly so that they feel that the meal is an important social event in their day. Institutions are sometimes too economical about table settings. A number of relatively inexpensive plastic fabrics now on the market make practical and at the same time decorative table coverings. Table coverings are not an expensive budgetary item and should not be sacrificed to false economy.

The same is true with silverware, dishes, and platters. There must be enough attractive dinnerware so that children can feel attracted by the setting itself. While the setting of the table can be delegated to some of the children, it should not be relinquished to them. The child-care worker must participate actively in this process. Actually the child-care worker can teach the children to set the table invitingly. During the spring and summer, flowers might be placed on the tables. The chairs must be comfortable, and the space between the individual chairs wide enough to avoid unnecessary disorder.

Serving the meal itself presents a number of problems for several reasons. Sometimes there are so many children in the group that by the time the last ones are served, the meals of the first are cold (or have been consumed). Children's attention span, their ability to wait for each other, is limited. One cannot expect a hungry child with a plate full of food before him to wait until fifteen other meals are served. It is important that the food be distributed as quickly as possible. While children can wait for second servings until the others have consumed their first portions, this waiting is not easy with the first portion. In some cases the assistance of some of the more mature children can be a help. With the younger groups it might be necessary to have the food on the plates before the children are called to the table, so that they do not have an unnecessarily long waiting period.

It is most advisable for the adult to eat with the children. It not only brings to this joint eating some of the family atmosphere but also it demonstrates to the children that there is no special food for the adult. However, in view of the turmoil during mealtime, and in view of the adult's own needs for adequately served meals, and the fact that the children need his attention during meal times, under certain circumstances it is easier for all concerned if the adults do not eat some meals with the children, although they must always sit with them during meals. This is especially true if the adult has to take care of more than four or five younger children at the dinner table.

Should the adult serve the food or should the children serve themselves from platters? This depends on the age. For younger children meals should be served. Serving on platters might be more desirable for older children, provided that every child gets his share. Even in this case it is advisable that some food be served directly by the child-care worker. Since at the institution the adults do not provide the food by preparing it, they have to assume part of the maternal function of giving food by serving it.

Table Manners

Table manners are not learned by a set of rules, but by imitation. Children imitate their parents' table manners. Often parents have to remind the children of the importance of table manners. If children have not acquired table manners by adolescence, this lack is very difficult to overcome. Children who come to the institution not only show a greater lack of table manners than other children, but also have sometimes reached an age when it is difficult to learn by imitation. One imitates people whom one likes and wants to identify with. That is why children imitate the adults they like. Children who come to the institution do not have any particular relationship to the people at the institution, and therefore have little motivation to imitate them. This prevents their adopting good table manners. They are often more eager to imitate each other than to imitate the adult in the unit, so that frequently one finds that individual children's table manners become worse rather than better at the institution. The child-care worker who insists on good table manners often is resisted by the whole group, who may see in him the nagging, ungiving disciplinarian rather than the food-providing parent figure. Nevertheless, insistence on a minimum of table manners is necessary. The child-care worker must demonstrate good table manners himself when he eats with the children. Younger children, if they accept the adult, will soon also accept his eating patterns and will follow his example. The other children resent the child-care worker's insistence on good table manners, but they usually try, after a fashion, to follow his demands for acceptable eating habits. If the child-care worker did not insist on the observance of certain rules at meals, they would be confused. Rules about manners must be simple, understandable, and easy to carry out.

A meal must have a beginning and an ending. Sometimes, in a family, the meal begins with a prayer, or with the mother sitting down to eat, or with the father giving some sign that the meal is starting. In an institutional group, the beginning must be impressive enough so that all the children know that the meal has started. In some institutions, a prayer or a blessing serves this purpose. Other forms or rituals can equally well mark the beginning of a meal, such as a little poem, a "saying of the day," or just the adult stating, "and now let us eat." This beginning ritual should not be long. The children's hunger instinct cannot be put to too great a trial.

Similarly at the end of the meal there must be some form of ritual. Again this might be a prayer or a poem, or just a very definite and brief statement on the part of the adult, such as "now we are through eating." The formal ending of the meal will prevent the children from rushing off wildly, thus destroying the group spirit that, it is hoped, existed during the meal.

It is as frustrating to a child to have to sit at a table after he is through eating, as it is to wait too long for a meal to begin. Mealtimes should be short in order to maintain a dignified atmosphere. While meals should be short, they should not be rushed. There are always some children who finish their meals before others, and others who eat so slowly that they detain the whole group. The child-care worker must see that the duration of the meal is realistic for all children. Most children cannot sit around a dinner table longer than fifteen to twenty minutes. All children should be expected to stay at the table for this period of time. Special consideration is necessary for exceptionally slow eaters, who should be allowed to stay on after the formal ending, so that they get the necessary pleasure and nutrition from the meal. Arrangements for the supervision of such slow eaters must be made. The other children should not be detained because of a few slow eaters. They would resent this and in one way or another "get even" with the laggards. Nor should the slow eaters be penalized because they are not through with their meals at a certain time. Dawdling over food is an important part of their personalities, and was often a source of friction and frustration in their own homes. It should not become such a conflict area within the institution.

Table Conversation

Relaxed table conversation is always a desirable accompaniment to eating. One cannot expect children to eat silently, nor would it be good for them. On the other hand, table conversation among children may deteriorate into yelling, shouting, sometimes even fighting. The child-care worker, therefore, must see that table conversation does not get out of hand. When children sit at different tables they should not make conversation from one table to another. When children sit at one long table the child-care worker should place himself where he can easily hear the children talk, so that shouting in order to reach him is unnecessary. Interesting conversation is a very helpful group formative tool. The child-care worker can encourage such conversation. He might ask questions. He might tell something about himself or he might stimulate the children to tell some of their own experiences during the day. If the conversation is interesting and the children are very much involved, they might remain seated around the dinner table until the conversation dies down.

Snacks

While this discussion has focused mostly on meals, it is important that institutions make available to children snacks and occasional refreshments outside regular mealtimes. Thus, bedtime snacks have been established in most institutions, if only because supper time is usually quite early and children get hungry again before they go to bed. Occasional servings of ice cream, cookies, and fruit are important. When children return from school they should get something to keep them satisfied until supper time. More important than the nutritional value is the personal aspect of these periodic snacks. When children return from playing on the ball field and find that the child-care worker has prepared a cold drink or small sandwiches, or perhaps some cake, they not only enjoy the food because they need it physically, but also because it is a concrete sign of the adult's interest in them. When Johnny, whose favorite dessert is chocolate pudding, finds that at his birthday party chocolate pudding is served, he not only enjoys the food but also the thought behind its preparation. Children who have been deprived of affection sometimes can accept it only in this tangible way. Spontaneous voluntary giving of food can become an excellent means of binding the child to the adult.

SUMMARY

The social value of food cannot be over-estimated. Food is one of the easiest social, educational and therapeutic tools that the child-care worker has at his disposal. While nutritional and budgetary factors must always be considered in organizing food in an institution, social factors have the greatest educational effect on the child. While the nutritional and pleasure values are mainly determined by the dietician and the administration, the psychological and social values of food are greatly the responsibility of the child-care worker, one in which he must not fail.

CHAPTER 4

The Day Has Twenty-four Hours

ROUTINES AND SCHEDULES

Every institution must organize the children's day so that their major physical, psychological, and social needs are adequately met. From getting up in the morning to going to bed at night, every child's day is filled with important events that, in the eyes of his parents and of society, are necessary to prepare him for healthy adulthood. Whether he brushes his teeth once, twice, or three times a day is determined partly by the standards of dental hygiene in his social group, partly by the emphasis parents put on these standards, and partly by his own readiness to abide by them. Similarly, whether or not he uses his free time to play a musical instrument depends on his social group, his parents and himself. The food he eats, the clothes he wears, the books he reads, the games he plays are all decided by these three determinants. The mother who is worried about germs will become more concerned about a child's failure to take a shower at night than the mother who does not believe in germs. But both mothers want their children to grow up and become healthy, happy, socially successful people. The daily living program of the children is geared toward this goal.

Institutional schedules and programs are directed toward the same end. However, the institution has children from many different backgrounds, cultures, and families and with many personality differences. The child-care worker is an important agent in the achievement of these aims. The daily program is the instrument by which these methods are applied and their progress measured. Furthermore, the social and philosophical beliefs of the authorities responsible for institutions—boards of trustees, government bodies, and executive directors—vary greatly. These variations are expressed in the program. Above all, the purpose of the institution brings about variations. Therefore, while the basic routines are very similar in all institutions, there are some significant variations determined by their functions. We will mention just four of them.

For instance, training schools deal exclusively with delinquent children committed by the court. The program must make it possible for these children to be controlled in order that they may be treated. Some institutions emphasize religious education more than others. Some (boarding schools in particular) regard college preparation as a major educational task. Finally, a growing number of institutions regard treatment of a child's emotional problems as their major function. These have particular social and clinical goals.

Institutions have different methods of achieving their goals. For instance, some institutions use militaristic techniques as a means of achieving greater socialization; others regard these methods as obsolete. These special functions of the institution influence its routines. While in the first group the daily routines might include a greater number of checks and roll calls, the second group will have more religious or educational activities, the third group more military activities, and the fourth group of institutions will gear their routines to the clinically established emotional needs of the individual child.

Nevertheless the similarities far outweigh the differences. It seems justified to discuss routines as basic to all institutions. Suggestions made here as to how routines can be best handled are not prescriptions. There is more than one way in which to do these things. We present ways which we have found most expedient and helpful.

All institutions are based on the assumption that education, treatment, and growing up are a twenty-four-hour-a-day business, so that everything in daily life becomes a means toward the goal of bringing about a healthy, well integrated, socially functioning individual. Many things that have to be done, like cleaning, laundering, and keeping the cottage in order are not important only for the smooth functioning of the institution, but also for the smooth functioning of the child himself now and in the future. The child-care worker has to help the child see the connection between helping straighten out the living room and becoming a better adjusted person. If there is no connection between these two goals there is question as to whether routine is necessary. When the child-care worker learns in a conference that a child is compulsively clean, or is hysterically fearful about his health, or has a "school phobia," these diagnostic classifications are meaningful to him only if he can project them into the framework of daily living. How does the child's pathology affect his relationship to the child-care worker and to his peers? How does it affect his attitude to his allowance, his chores in the cottage, his school work? How can the child-care worker help him in these areas? Only as they apply to everyday life do diagnostic classifications, casework recommendations, and psychiatrist's consultations make sense to the child-care worker, and only then do they become essential. In too many institutions the road from the psychiatrist's office to the dormitory seems interminably long. Yet the ultimate success of institutional treatment depends on how clinical findings can be applied to everyday living.

In discussing the outline for the twenty-four hours of the day we are aware that it is not so important that everything go according to this outline. It *is* important that the outline itself is in accordance with the spirit that pervades the total institution. This spirit should be one of enjoyment of orderly living. The events of the day should not be obstacles to the child's search for fun. This spirit is achieved— as we stated in the preceding chapters—by the total atmosphere of the institution, by satisfactory relationships to understanding adults and by the feeling of belonging to the peer group. Everything said about the routines of the day has to be seen in this light. The child-care worker cannot fulfill the functions confronting him during the twenty-four hours of the day just by having an outline of what to do and what not to do. He has to know that a great deal of what he can expect from the children depends on the totality of their life experiences before and during their stay at the institution.

Getting Up

The rising hour should be planned so that the children have adequate time to get ready for the day. Some institutions have a tendency to awaken the children earlier than necessary. Sometimes the convenience of a cook or maid or a laundry worker has more influence on rising time than the needs of the children or the program. In an average family, a child gets up not earlier than an hour before he has to leave for school. In institutions this should be sufficient too. It may be that in winter, when children have to dress more completely, the rising time should be a little earlier than in summer.

Should all children rise at the same time? Most institutions function on the principle that they should. The routines, such as meals and chores, seem to point to the need for a uniform rising time. On the other hand, some institutions have been able to operate effectively with a more flexible plan. This permits the children to get the maximum of sleep. Breakfast need not be a group meal but can be taken individually. The breakfast period should be extended until all the children have eaten. This is simple where individual cottages are equipped with dining facilities. Even institutions with central dining halls have arranged breakfast cafeteria style over a longer period of time. This enables the children to arise according to their own schedules.

To the child-care worker it seems at times that there are two kinds of children in institutions—those who get up before they should, and those who don't get up when they should. Very often the supervisors of younger groups complain that the children get up too early, while on the other hand the people in charge of adolescent groups complain constantly that they have a difficult time getting the youngsters out of bed.

Everyone who has been away from home against his own will, whether in the army, in a hospital, or elsewhere, knows what it is like to awaken among strangers. The sudden impact of the situation can be unbearable. The rudeness of the awakening can be aggravated by the call of the bugle, by the vindictive shouts of an army sergeant, or by the unfriendly act of a grouchy night nurse pushing a thermometer into your mouth. In an institution children wake up in the morning and are confronted with an unpleasant reality—the fact that they are not home with their parents. Who knows what their dreams were during the night? Perhaps they dreamt of a nice home with comfort, pleasure, and love. Some children need longer than others to find their way back to reality. Waking the children, therefore, should always be done in a sensitive and kind fashion. Redl and Wineman reported that in their institutions the housemother went into the children's room a half hour before rising time, made herself busy and told the children when they awoke that they could stay in bed for a while, instead of getting up immediately.

It is best to wake the children individually. The child-care worker might go over to each child and say in a friendly and clear voice, "Good morning, Jack. Time to get up." The experienced child-care worker can usually anticipate how the individual child will react to being awakened. Some children resent bodily contact like a tap on the shoulder. Some might have to be called repeatedly, while others might have to be whispered to. The person who wakes up the children ought to be fully dressed and well groomed, and, it is hoped, conveying the joy of being awake. The child in an institution should feel that the person who wakes him up enjoys being awake himself. Therefore, the child-care worker should give himself time to get fully ready before he wakes up the children. Any mechanical awakening, such as whistles, bells, or even alarm clocks are too impersonal and cannot replace the personal human touch. They should not be used. Only after other methods fail and the child refuses to get up should more forceful methods be applied. First, however, it should be established whether a child is sick or has any other reason for not getting up. The child-care worker might have to sit on his bed and find out what is wrong. Only after this is done may he force the child, after first preparing him for it. He might say, "I hate to do this but it's time to get up now. I can't give you any more time. I've called you four times already. Now I'm going to pull your blankets off." Then he may proceed to carry out his plan. The variations of this method can be manifold, but the spirit should always be one of softness and personal interest **without anger and punitiveness.**

Personal Hygiene

STANDARDS AND VARIATIONS

Personal hygiene is an important part of the schedule.

MOTHER: "Johnny, you didn't wash your hands."
JOHNNY: "I did."
MOTHER: "They're dirty."
JOHNNY: (*Showing part of his hand*) "No, they're clean."
MOTHER: "No, they're dirty, wash them again."
JOHNNY: "No, I won't!"

This little scene occurs every day in thousands of families all over the world, between well adjusted children of all ages and their mothers, but it occurs most frequently with children between the ages of nine and thirteen. Mothers have been trying for years to impose their standards on children, but discover that in the matter of personal hygiene they have been painfully unsuccessful. Nostalgically, they look back to the time when they really could control their child's cleanliness, when they were small enough to be washed if they did not wash themselves. At five, Johnny thought it was fun to practice with the toothbrush. He enjoyed sitting in his bath and getting himself just as clean as mother did, even a little cleaner. He insisted that he could do everything all by himself, even cut his toenails. At ten, all this has changed. He seems completely absorbed in other activities. He has no time to wash himself. He rinses his hands and barely moistens his face. His fingernails are always dirty, his hair disheveled. Mothers need not be discouraged—at the age of thirteen or fourteen, he will suddenly take more interest in cleanliness and may even become a little particular about his hair and general appearance.

If parents who had all the opportunities to influence the child and control his development throughout the years have such difficulties in maintaining standards of personal hygiene with their own children, one can imagine how much more difficult it is for substitute parents, counselors, foster parents, and institutional child-care workers, who have not known the child during the past, to establish standards. These must, nevertheless, be set and maintained. Institutional child-care workers have to keep in mind that children's resistance to personal hygiene does not reflect on them as individuals. Some of the children actually come from homes with low hygienic standards, but one cannot assume this about all children who disregard standards of cleanliness. For a child in an institution, the normal resistance to cleanliness may be complicated by many factors. He may want to demonstrate his worthlessness by disregard for his appearance. He may also want to test the child-care worker's interest and authority. Does he care enough? Can he make me? With the institutional child another motivation may unconsciously be operating. He may do this to punish his parents for having sent him away, by showing the world what a "dirty" family he came from. In the area of personal hygiene a few simple rules may be helpful—some minimal requirements for personal hygiene which everybody can fulfill.

Washing in the morning, before meals, and before going to bed should be required for each child. Washing in the morning should be thorough. Showers or baths should be substituted for washing in the evening at least every other day. Facilities for washing should be easily available. There have to be enough faucets so that the children need not wait for each other. Towels should be provided with individual name tags, so that a child feels that his towel is really his. Soap should be easily available, possibly individualized. Space to keep these items should be provided near the child's bed or in the bathroom.

Some institutions give baths to younger children once or twice a week. Others have showers daily or every other day. On the whole a simple rule applies: when the child is dirty, he should clean up, or should be cleaned. Children in an institution do not have to be cleaner than children outside, but they should not be dirtier. The child must have the feeling at all times that rules of cleanliness are enforced in his own interest. If a youngster returns from the pool, and has had a shower before and after swimming, it is not necessary for him to take another shower just because the schedule orders it. On the other hand, if a child dirties himself shortly after taking a shower it might be advisable for him to take another.

Sufficient shower stalls are necessary to permit privacy as well as supervision to keep homosexual excitement at a minimum. Special attention should be given to some children who do not want to expose themselves to other children in the nude.

Bathroom facilities should be easily accessible to the children. Enough toilets should be available on all floors where children spend their time, and especially where they sleep. Sometimes children wait too long to interrupt an activity before they rush to the toilet. All toilet facilities should provide privacy, so that no unnecessary embarrassment takes place. The normal toilet habits of each child should be observed by the child-care worker. Any persistent irregularity should be taken up with the nurse and supervisor. Children who suffer from enuresis (wetting) and encopresis (soiling) are in special need of discreet handling. These conditions usually result from inner unhappiness. Children suffer a great deal from these habits, although at times they deny it. These children must be protected from ridicule, embarrassment, or punishment. In only a few children is this disorder the result of lack of training. All these children need understanding encouragement, and faith rather than annoyance and threats. The handling of such children's laundry should not be left up to them, but should be so managed that they do not feel discriminated against. A container in which they can put their soiled laundry and linen should be available. The child-care worker's accepting, kindly attitude is a crucial factor in the recovery of these children from these disorders. The caseworker should always be informed of the disorder and of the child's reaction to it.

Daily dental care is necessary as part of the personal hygiene which the child has to learn. The child-care worker has to help the child to carry out this part of his daily health program. An adequate supply of attractive tooth brushes, and individual choice and possession of dentifrice can help achieve this goal. It is important to remember that in this area, as in so many others, the child-care worker is responsible for helping the child establish patterns which will serve him throughout his life.

Supervision of the personal hygiene program is necessary even in those cases where the child carries it out more or less independently. While children might express resentment about checking and "nagging," they really expect and need it. Younger children need help in many of these areas, and older children in some.

Cleaning ears, arranging hair, cleaning and cutting finger and toe-nails, arranging for hair cuts, are all steps in developing from dependency to self-reliance. They have to be taken one at a time as the child is ready. Children often overestimate their readiness for these things, and really need more help than they admit. The child-care worker has a twofold objective: to help the child establish habits of personal hygiene for himself, and to maintain good standards for him until he can carry them out himself. On the whole, supervision of personal hygiene is a "mother's function," and therefore it is preferable that at least one mature woman child-care worker be in each group. While not all children can accept mothering in this area, most of them want it. Direct application of motherliness is possible, and in most cases desirable, with younger children. With older children, a more subtle attitude is advisable.

It is very important, since growing children have many questions about their sexual development, that the person who gives the control and support is a person of the same sex. It is important that the child-care worker sees the children in the nude occasionally in order to know whether their development is progressing normally. Any abnormality should be brought to the attention of the supervisor and the nurse.

Most important, of course, is the availability of a mother person for girls during their pubic development preceding menstruation, to give them the facts about the necessary hygiene and emotional assurance about this startling, frightening biological process. A clear and early explanation, a casual and secure attitude, availability of supplies, and motherly understanding are needed by the girls of this age.

Health

No matter how many health specialists there are in an institution, it is important that the child-care worker be the guardian of a child's health and physical care. It is he to whom physical distress and abnormal physical reactions first become known. These might occur in the morning when the child wakes up, in the daytime, or in the middle of the night. It is he who has to know what to do in case of an accident or an emergency. He can usually recognize whether a child is really sick or pretending, whether he is minimizing his pains or exaggerating them. It is he who helps the child take the medicine that has been prescribed, who supervises any special diet that has been ordered. It is he who watches the child before the sickness comes, protects him from overeating, undereating, over exertion, or sleeplessness.

To be sure, every institution needs health specialists. It is essential to have an adequate health department under the supervision of a qualified pediatrician, who not only understands pediatrics, but also the special needs of the children.

It is neither possible nor necessary to have a full-time pediatrician on the staff of most institutions. An attending pediatrician who is readily available and a well qualified nurse are usually sufficient. Specialists and a hospital must be available for cases of serious illness. As for minor illness and epidemics, the large institution usually has its own infirmary where children can be cared for. The use of the infirmary depends greatly on the policy of the institution, its physical structure, and its staff schedules. It is desirable that children with mild, but not infectious illness remain in their own units whenever possible, for during sickness they most need those people to whom they are accustomed. A transfer to the unaccustomed environment of the infirmary is especially hard to take and might be interpreted as rejection. Their physical illnesses are aggravated by the feeling of desertion and loneliness. Against this, however, must be considered the element of contagion, the disturbance that such an illness might present to the rest of the children, the amount of care a child can get in the unit. The fact that an institution might have a special medical department does not relieve the child-care worker of the responsibility for his health. If, the moment the child complains of not feeling well, the child-care worker tells him to go see the nurse and does not show concern for his complaints, he abandons the child at a very difficult time. At times of illness children miss their mothers most. An adult usually remembers, of his childhood diseases, not the sickness itself, but how he was the center of attention at the time, how the whole family tiptoed around his bed, and how mother seemed to be available exclusively for him. In the institution one takes away from children this important gratification which they find in illness, by sending them to the infirmary. It is important that a child recognizes that his being sick distresses the adult. The child-care worker can express regret for having to move him to another place and can show him that he would want to be with him in this difficult period. Certainly the child-care worker should accompany the child to the infirmary, rather than send him there. This is true even for the older child. He has to show his interest while the child is at the infirmary, by visiting with him and sympathizing with his discomforts.

When a child's illness becomes apparent in the morning, although the child-care worker is busy with the other children, he should check the child quickly and tell him to wait in his bed or on a chair until the child-care worker is through with the others and can give more attention to him. This depends, of course, on the emergency nature of the illness. It also might depend on what time the doctor comes, so that the child will not miss the doctor's visit. It is always important for the child-care worker to encourage and support the child during illness, not to frighten him with any of the possible consequences of his illness, to understand his fears and anxieties about it, and to try to help him face the medical care that he must undergo.

All illness is connected with anxiety, often physical pain, and fear of death. It is important that the people responsible for his psychotherapeutic treatments are immediately notified when a child becomes ill. In cases of serious illness the child's parents or guardian should be informed immediately. This is usually the responsibility of the caseworker who deals with them. In addition to real physical disease there is always a good deal of neurotic sickness and pretended ailments. A child might use a physical disorder or a pretended one (putting a penny in the mouth to raise the temperature) to avoid some painful experience during the day, or to gain special attention. It is a well known fact that institutional children are more frequently ill during school days than during holidays. These neurotic manifestations and pretenses require special handling. Such situations should be discussed with the child's supervisor and his therapist.

It is always necessary that one recognize that behind this deception is anxiety, and that while the child might not really have a stomachache he might be bothered by some homework which he has not done, by the ostracism he is facing in school, or by a task he thinks he cannot achieve during the day.

When one cannot accept at face value a child's complaint of illness, one has to support him in his anxiety, which arises from another area of his life. While one has to distinguish real illness from pretended illness, it is sometimes safer for the child to feel that he might be able to get away with a complaint of illness than to feel that everyone suspects him. It might also be safer physically to give the child the benefit of the doubt sometimes, even though one is suspicious, rather than possibly to neglect to recognize real illness when it occurs. Only in exceptional cases are we faced with malingering, which can be dealt with by "calling the child's bluff," denying him the escape into sickness.

Medical instructions to the child-care worker have to be carried out meticulously. If the child has to follow a medical regime the child-care worker must supervise it and make sure that it is carefully followed. Inability to follow it or to gain the child's cooperation should be reported immediately. Health records are usually the responsibility of the caseworker or the medical personnel.

Clothing

When the child gets up in the morning he should find the clothing he is to wear during the day in a special place near his bed arranged in an orderly way. The clothing should be in good condition, clean, and appropriate to the use the child is to make of it. It should have been prepared the evening before. With the younger age group this is mainly the job of the child-care worker. Even the youngest child should know what he is to wear and participate to the best of his ability in selecting his clothing. Older children can prepare their clothing themselves, but inconspicuous checking by the adult is almost always necessary, as a reminder of a forgotten item, or of a decided change. Interest in the child's clothing can be an important aid in establishing a relationship between the child-care worker and the youngster.

The time allowed for getting dressed should be sufficient for the average child. There are children who dress quickly and children who dress slowly. Some of the best daydreams occur between the sock and the left shoe. There is Johnny sitting and holding his left sock in his hand, apparently totally absorbed in thought. Jackie, who started later, is already dressed and ready for breakfast. The child-care worker has to make allowances for the slow Johnnies and the speedy Jacks. He must be on hand to admonish one, encourage another, praise a third, and assist a fourth. While children who are very upset or who have special handicaps may need assistance in dressing, the goal should be to enable all children to dress themselves.

THE MEANING OF CLOTHING

Clothing in our society has three major purposes: to protect the body from weather and other hazards; to indicate a person's belonging to a social group; and to distinguish the individual from others in his group.

While, except for a few professions, such as the military, the police, certain religious and other services, clothing does not officially indicate a person's rank in society, it still indicates that he is a part of a social group. The kind, quality, combination, style and value of his dress give conspicuous if sometimes misleading evidence of an individual's social class and role. At the same time it shows his individuality and personal drives, his desire to be important and different from everyone else. With children (and with most adults) the desire to be dressed like everyone else in the group is usually greater than the desire to be individually different. The desire to be alike is especially great among youngsters from the age of six to twelve. It changes slowly, so that by the age of fifteen one usually has a greater desire to be different. By and large, most children in institutions fall into the age group where children definitely want to be dressed like their peers. Younger children disregard the purpose and value of clothing altogether; their preoccupation is with activity rather than form, with locomotion rather than appearance.

It is essential that each child in the institution have individual

clothing, which is definitely his property, and it is equally important that every child have individual space to keep his clothing.
Non-seasonal clothing can be stored away. This individualization
is even more essential in the institution than in a family, for in the
latter the child is much more the center of attention. Clothing
contributes to a child's developing a feeling of his own identity.
This is shown especially in the way a child cares for the clothing
given him by parents and·relatives as compared to his disregard
of the clothing given to him by the institution. While the distribution of clothing in an institution cannot give the child the same
feeling of pride and identity, it has to stress the individuality and
private ownership of clothing in every child.

All children should arrive at the group living unit of the institution with an adequate supply of clothing comparable to that of
the other children. This can be arranged by establishing a list of
required clothing at the time of admission. If these requirements
cannot be met by the parents, the referring agency or the institution itself should meet them. Basic clothing should be chosen so
that the children can feel suitably dressed and individualized rather
than uniform.

Maintenance of Clothing

An institution must have sufficient laundry and sewing facilities
to guarantee that the children can dress properly and adequately.
While it is not the child-care worker's basic function to do the
sewing and laundry, he is responsible for seeing that it is done
quickly and efficiently. Looking over the clothing with the child
periodically, seeing that torn clothing is sent to be mended, that
soiled clothing is sent to be laundered or cleaned, and checking
clothing coming back from the laundry to see that it is in adequate
condition, is as important an act of "motherly" love as any. The
child can sense the care, interest, and protection of an adult in this.

In some institutions the child-care workers do the mending, but
most institutions have a sewing room. Its existence however, should
not prevent the child-care worker from occasionally doing some
mending or darning for the child directly. Every child sometimes

has a very urgent need to have a button sewed on, or a rip mended. It would be outright rejection if the child-care worker would refuse to help at such a point by "referring" the child to the sewing room. Maintenance of clothing is something especially complicated because the children's neglect of clothing affects not only their appearance but also the institutional budget.

When a child returns from school the clothing he is expected to change into should be available to him. While it is difficult enough to get children to change their clothing, it is more difficult if they have to search for the play clothes they are supposed to wear for the rest of the day. The child-care worker has to have time to prepare for these changes, so that when the child is asked to change his clothing, he find its easy to fulfill the request.

It is important that adolescents learn to maintain their clothing themselves. While individual variations are necessary, an effort should be made to help girls learn to wash their own lingerie. Adolescent boys also might learn to wash some of their clothing if necessary, or to iron their trousers. Convenient facilities for such self-service should be available in each group living unit.

An institution must have in its budget funds for replacement of clothing. Children outgrow and outwear their clothing. Whenever possible, replacements should provide the child with new clothing. Sometimes institutional budgets make this impossible, and some of the clothing children get has been worn by other children. This has to be handled very sensitively, so that the children's self-respect is not hurt. Clothing purchases should always be individualized, even if the clothing is purchased centrally. Acquiring new clothing should be a joyous event for the individual child, one he can look forward to. His participation in selecting or buying new clothing should be solicited, even if his judgement is still limited in this area. Older children can participate in planning and selecting their wardrobes more fully, until finally they can do it themselves. In the selection of clothes special attention should be paid to physically exceptional children—those suffering from obesity, visible birthmarks, or posture deformities. The more these children can be helped to look attractive, the easier it is for them to accept themselves and their conditions. Sometimes special budgetary allocations are necessary for these children, since they cannot always use standard clothing. The child-care worker, by helping them to obtain the most adequate and attractive attire and to see themselves less as exceptions, helps them to move from a state of isolation and differentness toward social participation.

Age Differences and Clothing

Children from the ages of six to twelve usually regard any regulations about clothing, such as clothing changes after school or special Sunday clothing, as necessary evils imposed by adults. They do not really understand them. They are more preoccupied with activities than with appearances. It is not a willful disrespect for dress or for adults who insist on proper attire that makes them neglect their clothing, but their own preoccupation. Other things have priority in their minds. Mothers, as well as child-care workers, often expect too much from children in this age group. They think the children can "take care" of their clothing. In reality they must constantly be helped and reminded. Sometimes these reminders take the form of battles between the adult and the child, not so much because the child questions and resists the adult's authority, but mainly because changing his clothing interrupts some other activity in which he is more interested. While these "battles" cannot be completely eliminated they can be largely avoided. The adult should recognize the child's resistance as stemming from his absorption in other activities, and should firmly and kindly insist on the necessary clothing changes. These changes are necessary during this period of time; otherwise the life expectancy of clothing would be too short for most families, and certainly for most institutional budgets. As a matter of fact the child expects the adults to remind him and reprimand him about his clothing, and would be confused and insecure if they did not.

In this area, as in that of personal hygiene, the child-care worker is a parent figure, more specifically a mother figure. It is important for children of this age group that there be a woman on the child-care staff who can help them develop good clothing habits. Enough play clothing that can take hard wear and tear should be available for these children. While constant assistance of the adult is necessary, it is important that the child be slowly trained to take responsibility for his clothing himself. While a child at this age probably disregards some of the standards that the adults set, at a later age he will remember them. They actually might then become the foundation of his clothing habits for the rest of his life.

It is helpful to know whom or what the child wants to dress up for. Even if he wants to be like the peer group, it does not necessarily mean that he wants to dress up for them. Younger children do not pay much attention to each other's clothing. A younger child's desire is usually to please the adult. He is very proud if he meets with the adult's approval. It is helpful to recognize who the specific adult is in a group living unit whom the child would like to please most with his clothing. It might be visiting parents, one of the cottage counselors, the caseworker, or a teacher. In order for a child to feel that his efforts are worthwhile, it is mandatory that when he is nicely dressed adults who are important to him notice and comment favorably on his appearance.

From the age of twelve on, the situation becomes more complicated, because then it is not a child's forgetfulness and preoccupation which make him disregard the adult standards. It is actually his inner resistance toward these standards that makes him so conspicuously (although usually unconsciously) neglect his clothing. This is the age when suddenly one finds a child's clothing lying all over the floor, when one shoe is in one corner and the other in another, when children dress inappropriately by adult standards, and when they resent being reprimanded or "nagged."

They still need help with their clothing, but they do not want to acknowledge this help; indeed, they resent it and fight against it. This is a very difficult period for all mothers, and, of course, for all child-care workers.

A child between twelve and sixteen years wants to be like and look like his peers. Very often he wants to impress a member of the opposite sex. During this time greater attention is given to clothing of peers. They observe each other's clothing carefully and make critical comparisons. This is especially true of girls. Yet the adult's criticism of the peers' dress often has a negative effect. It provokes the youngster to come to the defense of his peers, although he might himself disapprove of their dress. Girls devote a great deal of time discussing clothing problems. The adult must take an interest in their problems, especially in the obvious desire to attract members of the opposite sex by their clothing. Some girls need encouragement in expressing these justified desires. They deny that they want clothing to attract boys, and they might be helped to feel that this purpose is not delinquent and bad, but normal and acceptable. On the other hand, some girls need to be checked lest they exceed the limits of decency and social order in their attire.

The child-care worker must patiently and consistently help the adolescent to dress properly. The economic value of clothing can slowly be interpreted by setting up individual clothing budgets. The youngsters should know the exact amount of clothing or money available during a given period of time. They should be helped to inventory their clothing supply and plan for replenishment on the basis of the available budget.

Adolescents go through a phase when their identification with their peer culture group frequently results in their dressing in seemingly inappropriate and unattractive clothing. During this phase adolescent girls walk around in blue jeans and men's shirts. They offend many a mother's esthetic sense and give adults the feeling that they make voluntary Cinderellas out of themselves. Nevertheless there is not much one can do about it. An institution can insist and require that a certain amount of conventional clothing be included in the basic clothing supply. It can also require that only conventional clothing be worn at certain times and places (dinner, movie attendance, chapel). However, institutions cannot swim against the stream of the culture. While the child-care worker can advise the youngster to choose proper clothing, he need not be surprised or distressed about some of the extravagances and oddities of adolescent taste.

Various committees can be established in which the adolescent can participate in setting clothing policies. Such questions as, What is an adequate clothing supply? How can clothing regulations be most effectively set up and implemented? How can laundry, sewing room and other facilities be utilized to serve the children's need most adequately?, all furnish good material for group discussion and action. The child-care worker who encourages their participation not only helps to promote greater group cohesion but also helps the individual children to more mature judgement and independence. Clothing is an excellent area in which one can mobilize the adolescent's desire for self-government. One can ask the adolescent to work out what kind of clothing he would want and how he would want to have clothing purchases administratively arranged.

No matter which age group he is dealing with in matters of purchase, selection, organization of cleaning and maintaining clothing, the child-care worker should try to give the child the feeling that behind all his reminding and training about clothing lies his real desire to have the child look attractive and respectable, because he believes he is worthwhile.

Chores

In most institutions children participate in some work. Usually chores are established with two considerations in mind: the educational value for the child, and the economic value for the institution. These two considerations are not necessarily mutually exclusive. On the contrary, work that is practical and economical often has also a certain educational effect. Children work more readily when they see that their work has a practical value. Nevertheless the economic consideration has to be a secondary one, lest they resent their chores and regard them as "slave labor." Some institutions are more interested in the economic than in the educational aspect of work and have thereby given a certain justification to the children's resistance to their chores.

There are three kinds of chores: (1) those the child does more or less for his own immediate benefit; (2) those the child does for the benefit of his immediate group living unit (the cottage or the dormitory); and (3) those he does for the institution at large.

These chores include making one's bed, cleaning one's locker, and sweeping one's room. They are an extension of personal hygiene. Most children can do some of them, but very upset children need help with them. Doing these chores require a desire on the part of the child to take care of himself but do not require great readiness to be a part of the group. Isolates, too, can do such chores and usually will do them satisfactorily. It is wisest to start with chores that children can do easily, which take only a few minutes of time. Workers in institutions sometimes forget that most young children in their own homes do not participate much in the upkeep of the home, and that even such chores as making one's bed are usually assumed much later in a family than is expected in an institutional setting. At home a child very often starts his work by helping his mother in something which is not at all connected with his own immediate needs, something which he enjoys doing, such as helping in the kitchen or shopping—chores in which he can identify with his parents. In an institution this does not occur often enough. The child does not have these opportunities for relationship to adults and such participation in the adult's job is not appealing enough to him. Some child-care workers can get the child interested in their own work. A counselor whom the youngsters like will have a whole group of children ready to help him when he repairs his car. Seeing him work will stimulate the children to develop good work habits themselves. Usually, however, this is not possible; therefore, chores should start with the child's concern for himself.

The adult has to praise the children for the accomplished work and thus instill pride in their own achievement and in the upkeep of their quarters.

Since belonging to a social group is an important part of their development in the institution, it is justifiable to have the children participate to a degree in the upkeep of their units. Such chores as sweeping the hall or the living room of the cottage, setting the dining room table, watering plants, picking up papers are common in most institutions. Many children do not like them. Children prefer play and hate the interruption of their play. Their resistance to chores often expresses their resistance to being at the institution. While many hostile children do not actively participate in destructive deeds against the institution, they express their hostility by passive resistance. Very often their chores are done negligently. Only as children feel that the living unit is theirs, that they belong, that the adults like them and want them to be there do they take pride in their living quarters. Only then are they able to do the chores with greater eagerness and efficiency. They can reach this stage, however, only if they have a positive feeling toward the child-care worker. It is important that in the living unit children are not substitutes for maids, and that the work to which they are assigned is relatively easy to do in a short time. The sacrifice they have to make of their own free time should not be so great that it evokes hostility and active or passive resistance. It is not advisable to expect children under ten to participate in these group chores.

Chores for children between ten and thirteen should be based on their educational needs rather than on the household and maintenance needs of the unit. The child-care worker's attitude toward their resisting work ought to be casual and matter-of-fact. He understands and expects the resistance, but he still has to insist that certain chores be done. He may explain to the children why they have to be done, he must see that the chores are distributed fairly, but he does not allow the children to neglect or ignore them. He sees to it that they do not take up an unusual amount of time. Fair distribution of chores does not mean equal chores for all children or an automatic rotation of chores. "Fair" means being fair to the individual child. Some children in each group are not ready to do any chores at a certain time, and some children can do more work than others. A group-rejected isolate, for instance, should not be given a chore on which the whole group depends, such as setting the table. If he is slow and delays the meals, he not only proves again his own inefficiency, he also increases group hostility toward himself. He should be given a chore as independent of the other children's activities as possible, such as cleaning the hall closet. Sometimes children have a rigid concept of fairness with regard to work which is actually a distortion of reality. Since not all children are equal, chores cannot be equal either. The child-care worker has to explain this. As he establishes a relationship with them, they recognize that he himself is fair, and likes them all, and will be able to invest more of themselves and get more pleasure from their work and from improving the appearance and the efficiency of their living unit.

Some institutions assign chores outside the children's own living units. This has to be done with utmost care. Unless they are a part of a regular training program which is a substitute for school or for other forms of training, or unless they are paid workers, it is highly questionable whether such chores have any educational value. As part of a systematic training program, of course, they are very important. As part of assigned regular work in addition to a child's educational program, they might be too much. In the section on "Work" the question of paid work outside the living unit will be discussed.

Supervising Chores

All children's work has to be supervised, whether it is done for themselves, for the living unit, or for the total institution. When the chore is satisfactorily completed, the child-care worker should show appreciation. If the chore is unsatisfactorily completed, the child-care worker should express his criticism in the most constructive way possible. In many cases when the work is done unsatisfactorily the child might have to do his chores again. However, because repetition may not improve the work, causing the child-care worker to become engaged in a vicious circle producing increasingly worse results, it might be wiser to explain to the child what is wrong, and to make the correction himself. The child-care worker might explain to the youngster that he does not seem to be ready to complete this assignment satisfactorily and that this unreadiness affects his general progress at the institution. An adolescent girl, for instance, who over a period of time has not yet learned to set a table right, might not be ready to go into a foster home or girls' club outside the institution. Or a child in a cottage of younger boys who is not able to make his own bed, might not be ready to be moved into an older boys' cottage, although this might be his wish. While the child-care worker should avoid a battle with the children about unsatisfactorily finished chores, he should under no circumstances accept negligently done chores as being correctly performed. This would impair the child's concept of reality and confuse him about the child-care worker's own standards.

The Timing of Chores

Most household chores are done in the morning. This means that between getting up, dressing, having breakfast and going to school the child has to squeeze in some work. Usually, these chores have to be very short so that under no circumstances do they adversely affect the child's relaxed approach to school. Chores which are done in the evening after mealtimes should also be as short as possible so that the child does not have to miss activities for long. No child under fourteen should spend more than thirty minutes on his total chores. Chores that take longer than this have the flavor of "labor" and interfere with other necessary activities. While it is not sound to pay children for regular chores within their living unit, it might be advisable to pay them for certain chores that take especially long or are unpleasant, for instance, dish washing or special cleaning up. In general, however, chores within the living unit should not be paid for and should be part of the child's responsibility as a member of the group.

Getting the Children Off to School

Sending children off to school is no minor task. Having finally gotten them out of bed, cleaned, and dressed, through their breakfast and their chores, the child-care worker has already done quite a job.

> When his child-care worker was just about sure that Johnny looked his best and was really clean, the boy ran out of the cottage and got himself all dirty. Quickly the child-care worker had to brush him, lest the school should again complain that Johnny came to school dirty, and that his child-care worker didn't seem to care for him.
>
> Then there was Joey, who forgot his arithmetic book yesterday and had a detention because of it. He almost forgot it again this morning, and the child-care worker had to run after him with the book and rush him to school.
>
> Jackie did not want to go to school in the first place. The child-

care worker tried first to persuade him, then to bribe him, and finally to threaten him with punishment.

These and many others are everyday occurrences in the child-care worker's life. When the children are all out of the unit, in school (or supposedly so) the child-care worker feels that he has done a full day's work.

Some institutions have their own schools. Here the problems are no less.

On the way from the cottage to the school Mark can get into mischief or get himself completely dirty. Although he leaves the cottage fifteen minutes before school time, and it takes him only two minutes to get there, he manages to come late. Melvin always has to run back because he forgets things.

In sending the children off to school the child-care worker has to identify with every child. He has to know when each child has to leave for school, what he needs to take along. He has to give a fresh handkerchief to one, money for lunch to the other, a bus ticket to the third. He has to remind one to take his geography book, another to comb his hair. In order to achieve all these tasks satisfactorily the child-care worker has to know each child's school problems. A few children like to go to school. However, most children at the institution have some school problems, usually of long standing. Going to school is an unpleasant experience for them. They leave the living unit with trepidation and anger; they need a lot of encouragement and support, and sometimes a little push. Institutional children attending school outside might easily feel stigmatized if their appearance, dress, or participation in activities differentiates them in any way from the other children. The child-care worker certainly cannot himself undo the emotional wounds that have been inflicted upon these children over the years. However, he can help the child in his appearance, in his punctuality, and by a friendly send-off. He has to help the child to have as much fun in going to school, and as little anxiety, as possible. If he listens interestedly to each child's school experience when the children come back from school he can anticipate the child's anxiety and know where he needs most support. Younger children and those who have difficulties in finding their way to school need to be escorted to school or to the school bus. It might be advisable for the child-care worker to go along and see that the children arrive at school as relaxed as possible. "Education" on the school bus should not be left to the bus driver, who has to concentrate on driving. These are some of the many tasks that the child-care worker has to perform in getting the children off to school and in setting the conditions for an enjoyable school experience.

Homemaking While the Children Are at School

After the children are all off to school, the child-care worker's responsibilities are not ended. Many things have to be done. Some of them, such as conferences with the supervisor or the caseworker and record keeping, will be discussed later in another chapter. The major content of the child-care worker's job during the hours between 9 A.M. and approximately 11 A.M. is making a "home" out of the living unit. During this time the child-care worker reviews the living unit, plans for the program and for the children. What did their behavior yesterday mean? What will they need today and tomorrow?

The child-care worker uses this time to bring structure and planning, warmth and beauty to the physical and emotional surroundings of the children. There are innumerable ways to achieve this goal; yet, one method is common to all good homemaking—organization and planning. Every child-care worker has to be an organizer.* Not every good mother is a good homemaker; in fact, some of the worst organizers can be excellent mothers. They have to compensate for their shortcomings in homemaking with other qualities. While the ability to establish relationships to children is the supreme requirement for all child-care workers, they have to be good homemakers too. This does not mean that in a unit in which there are two or three child-care workers, every one of them

* While we have used the masculine gender in reference to child-care workers, in this section we will refer to them in the feminine gender. It is difficult to detach the maternal function of child-care workers from their role as homemakers.

has to be a good housekeeper. A wise administrator will utilize the homemaking qualities of one child-care worker to supplement the leadership qualities of another. In every living unit there must be at least one good homemaker.

A good home must have an atmosphere of affection and understanding, good relationships among the members of the family and an organized daily schedule.

The atmosphere in each home is determined by many things, the way in which people make life convenient for each other, the comfort of the home, the respect that each member of the group has for another, and the fun people find in being with each other. Good relationships mean that people are ready to please and make life more enjoyable for one another, and to make sacrifices for one another. In a good home people anticipate each other's feelings and avoid hurting each other. In a good home people are liked not only for what they do but for what they are. There is no prescription for good relationships nor for a good home. They depend on inner feelings and personality. Yet there are certain conditions under which relationships can develop more readily and under which a home atmosphere may be more easily established. One of these conditions is organization of the home life. Organization gives people the feeling of security, protection, and comfort, all of them ingredients of the feeling of being loved.

The child-care worker has to use the time when children are away to organize the home, the living arrangements and the program of the children. She might go through the children's drawers to see if their laundry is in order, whether they have enough handkerchiefs or socks, whether some garments must be replaced, and others mended. She might look through the children's toilet articles to see whether Johnny needs a new cake of soap, or Jay a toothbrush. She might look around the space where the children sleep to see if their beds are comfortable, whether their mattresses have become lumpy or need new springs. She might wonder why some children have an abundance of pictures around their beds while others don't seem to have any, whether the space around the bed expresses the child's individuality. She might think of some decorations which she will suggest to one child. She might look to see whether each youngster has books, toys, or hobby material available. She might make a note to herself to see that John gets more crayons or some more stamps for his stamp collection. She might make sure that the children put away their dirty laundry, that shoes are shined and beds made. She may have to straighten out many a bed cover, rearrange a pillow here or a blanket there.

She might then go through the living room, dining room, and play room. She does not do all these things to check up on the children (she did that before they left) but to improve on what the children have done themselves. While children can do certain chores, they cannot be expected to become homemakers. They may have put the chairs in order around the table, but perhaps a few flowers on the table would embellish the home. They have set the table for dinner, but perhaps some colorful table mats or napkins would improve its appearance at mealtime. There may be a chair that needs upholstering. The child-care worker makes a note to tell the maintenance department about it. She reminds herself that the faucet in the kitchen leaks, and she must see that this gets repaired. She observed at breakfast that Johnny ate his grapefruit with a soup spoon. Are there enough teaspoons available? She might see. All these things contribute to the physical order of the home and cannot be done while the children are around. The child-care worker must have time for these things.

Furthermore, the children have their accounts. Yesterday Johnny received as a birthday present from his relatives, five dollars, which he gave to the child-care worker. Now she has to enter it on Johnny's account card. She gave Fred thirty-five cents this morning to buy a birthday card for his mother on the way to school. She has to take this off his account. There is the petty cash fund. She has to figure out how much money is left for entertainment for the month, how much money she can spend for the next birthday party. She must not forget to enter the two dollars she spent the evening before when the children went to the movies together.

More important than organizing the physical aspects of the children's affairs is organizing oneself. Part of the child-care worker's job is planning and thinking how to organize her own time. She needs a calendar in which she can note appointments, children's birthdays, and activities. She also needs a notebook in which to jot down things she has to discuss with her supervisor, the laundry, or sewing room manager. When the child-care worker in a cottage-plan institution goes to the administration building for mail, she might have twelve different things to look into at the same time. If she does not organize them and make some notes for herself she might have to make the trip between the cottage and the administration building five times instead of once.

If the child-care worker notices that Johnny needs new shoe-laces for his gym shoes and plans to get them today, she will not have an emergency the next morning. If she knows that the children are planning an outing and need transportation, she must make sure ahead of time that the bus is available. The best recreational activity could end in disaster if planning (and organization) did not precede it.

There are many practical things that the child-care worker has to do outside the living unit during these hours. She has to inquire of the sewing room whether the children's mending is done. She might have to go to the laundry to find out why certain things did not come back and whether some of the children can get quicker service because of special situations. While she cannot be responsible for doing the children's laundry, mending, and sewing, she is responsible for seeing that their clothing is well taken care of by the departments charged with this responsibility. Direct contacts with laundry personnel and seamstress are often necessary. Another important activity during this time is to get and send the children's mail.

While in general it does not seem possible for the child-care worker to go shopping for the children, nor advisable for him * to shop without them, there are occasions when things have to be purchased: a birthday present, underclothes, or knickknacks for the living unit.

The child-care worker can use the time when the children are in school to provide the little things that make life more livable. The little chores the child-care worker does such as rearranging chairs, picking up clothes, straightening out beds are important

* For convenience, all future reference to the child-care worker will be in the masculine gender.

ingredients of the warm atmosphere of the home. Children who come to the institution with hopelessness, hostility and fear of life, find the institution a little more attractive and life a little more pleasant. The little things become big things. The time the child-care worker devotes to these is well spent.

It is important that the child-care worker finds enough time to rest between the time the children go to school and the time they return. While all the things mentioned above are necessary, they should not take up all his free time. Child-care workers who work in split shifts also have to learn to sleep in split shifts, so that they do not become too exhausted. While a child-care worker has to be flexible about time, he must insist upon getting sufficient rest between work periods. The same is true for his privacy during his days off. While work at the institution is often fascinating and has a great impact on his personal life, the child-care worker must not sacrifice his privacy, and lose his own personal interests and avocations. Otherwise in the long run he will lose his healthy perspective with regard to his work and to life itself. This is especially true for resident child-care workers. Therefore, the free time of the child-care worker has to *be* free.

After School

When the children return from school the child-care worker and the unit must be ready for them. They should find living quarters and people ready to receive them when they come home. However they might not be ready either for contact with adults or their peers or for any scheduled activity. They may want to be "free." Every institutional program should make allowances for this desire.

The child-care worker should welcome every child individually. By empathy, anticipation, and a sensitive awareness of what the child's attitude might be, he can make the return from school as pleasant as possible and avoid unnecessary frictions. Above all, it is necessary that the child-care worker be present when the first child comes back from school. He must be free for the children and not preoccupied with other things. He should welcome every child in a way that is most appropriate to him. This might mean that he steps out of the building and picks up younger children at the school bus, or that he stands in front of the cottage and welcomes another youngster. In still another case he might ask immediately how a child did in a test, when he knows that the child had been concerned about the test. With another child he might carefully avoid discussing anything that happened in school. One child might bubble over to tell all about his experiences of the day, whereas another child simply cannot be bothered.

AFTER SCHOOL SNACKS

When children come home from school they are usually hungry and need a little snack that will keep them until suppertime, but not spoil their appetite for supper. A glass of milk, an apple, or a cookie might be sufficient and should be ready for them when they come. If each child could find his favorite snack ready when he comes home, he probably would feel most welcome and appreciated.

Mail

Children in an institution are eager to receive mail. One of the tragic scenes observed in a group is the reaction of those children who do not get mail when others do. Children should get their mail as soon after it arrives as possible. Whether the child-care worker gets the mail himself or whether it is sent into the living unit, it should always be distributed soon after it arrives. It is most helpful if the mail can be fetched while the children are at school, so that when they come back they find it waiting for them. Similarly, it is important that the letters children write are mailed quickly, preferably on the same day they are written, certainly not later than the next morning.

When children come home from school they are usually very eager to find out whether they had any mail. Mail has to be handled discreetly so as not to hurt those children who do not get any.

Although one cannot hide which children do get mail and which do not, the child-care worker has to find a way to distribute mail as quietly as possible. If one child gets a great deal of mail and another child gets none, it might be worthwhile to discuss it with that child's caseworker in order to help him. If a child receives letters that are regarded as undesirable or damaging, it is important that the child-care worker observes its effect on the child and discusses it with his caseworker and supervisor. In cases of unauthorized money or packages it might be necessary to open the mail before the child gets it and check for illegal content. In some rare cases it might be necessary to read the mail of these children before giving it to them.

Only after the child has had a pleasant welcome and is settled for a few minutes and after mail and snacks are distributed, is it advisable to insist on changing clothes. Children have to change from school clothing to play clothing after they come back from school, but they should not feel that the first words of welcome are, "go and change your clothes." Play clothes should be easily available so that the child does not have to overcome unnecessary hurdles in changing. If necessary, the child-care worker has to insist that a child change, and should help the younger children.

Individual Assignments

Between school time and suppertime it is desirable not to schedule any definite group program. Each child should use this time for special individual activities and for loafing. While much of the children's time in the institution is spent with the group, there must be sufficient time left for individual activities. Some children have hobbies, others are busy with their clothing, others like to read, and still others write letters home. There are the scheduled activities, such as contact with the caseworker, piano lessons, special tutoring, appointments with the doctor, the dentist, or the nurse, a psychological test, or a haircut. These individual appointments are usually scheduled in the period following school. The child-care worker must be aware of them and must remind the child of these commitments. Sometimes children need a little encouragement or even a little coercion in order to carry out these obligations. The child-care worker has to know when to use pressure and when to just remind a child of such appointments. He has to know how long the activity lasts and who supervises it. The child-care worker must have contact with the people who are dealing with the child during this time. Indeed, he must have contact with all the people who work with the child so that he knows how the child's behavior and attitudes outside the living unit compare with the behavior and attitudes within it. The child-care worker is responsible for the child during all the twenty-four hours of the day, even during those hours that he is not with the child. He must make sure that the child is never unsupervised, except in cases where it is planned for the child to be on his own.

More important than all these assignments and individual activities is the opportunity just to loaf. While a child always needs supervision, at this time supervision has to be as inconspicuous as possible. A child-care worker can supervise a youngster without being within three feet of him all the time, except in a few special cases. While a child needs organized activities it is even more important that he have time in which he can do anything or nothing. It is important for a child to feel that he does not have to be occupied all the time. He should be able to stretch out on a chair, the couch, his bed, or the grass in front of the building without being immediately told to do something. During this period of doing nothing he has to be watched unobtrusively, lest doing nothing deteriorates into doing something undesirable.

This is the time when the child-care worker has an opportunity for individual contacts with the children. He may discuss one child's allowance with him, or listen to children's stories about school, or help a youngster prepare for an evening costume party. He should be available during this time for any child who wants to be near him. He might also play some games with one of the isolates during this period. In addition to mealtimes this is the time when some special attention can be given to the isolate without evoking the hostility of the group.

Scheduled Activities

After the evening meal some scheduled activities are in order.
While these activities are planned and designed for the group, with
few exceptions they should not be compulsory, but should rather
have the relaxed, pleasant quality of voluntary participation.
There should always be somebody to take care of those children
who do not want to participate in these group activities. Scheduled
activities depend partly on the facilities, partly on the skill of the
adults who lead them, and partly on the group's interests. It is in
relation to such planned activities that voluntary group participation is most desirable and possible. Special discussion of recreational activities will follow in the section on Play and Recreation.

There are some unavoidable tasks, such as homework, mending,
and shoeshining, that have to be done. Although it is desirable that
they remain voluntary, it is sometimes easiest to set a certain time
aside, which the children are expected to use for these activities if
they have not already done them.

Homework

In older groups, homework is one of the scheduled activities. It is
advisable that in a unit of older children a period of an hour or so
be set aside for children to do their homework. Only after finishing
this should they be free for other activities. Children in junior
high school and high school usually have some homework to do.
It is necessary for the child-care worker to know enough about the
child's school activities to be able to supervise the child's homework. Some children are so anxious and eager about their homework that they start it immediately on their return from school,
and often forego any fun in order to finish their studying. These
children have to be encouraged to relax. Their anxiety about their
homework has to be reduced rather than increased. Most children,
however, need encouragement and perhaps slight pressure in order
to do their homework. It is always difficult to tear oneself away
from an enjoyable recreational activity and sit down to study,

especially if the subject is a troublesome one. It is important that during a homework period there are no other tempting recreational activities that would be distracting. For instance, if an exciting program is on the television set the children will not pay much attention to their homework.

If an important ball game is being played during the homework period, one cannot expect the children to concentrate on algebra. It might be necessary to expect all those children who have no homework to be inside the unit during this period, busying themselves with quiet activities, such as reading, writing letters home, or knitting. While one can force children to abide by a homework period one can seldom force them really to study. Some children who have trouble in doing their homework need encouragement and assistance. While the child-care worker does not have to be a specialist in any of the particular subjects, he has to be intellectually curious and alert enough to take a real interest in the child's school activities. Discussing the child's school work with him is necessary. The child-care worker has to be able to understand the child's work at school, his interests and his deficiencies. He has to be able to give praise when the child has done good work in school, but he should do this discreetly and not at the expense of the children who cannot compete in this area. To avoid embarrassing him he has to be able to reprimand a youngster tactfully for being negligent in his school work. Certainly no criticism should be directed at the child's intellectual limitations. The child-care worker need not give the impression that he is an expert in any subject. He can freely admit that there are many things he does not know. He must, however, recognize if and when Johnny needs some outside assistance, so that he can request tutoring for Johnny. The child-care worker's opinion is crucial in determining whether or not a child should get special tutoring.

Writing Letters

In some units a period is set aside in which the children can write letters to their parents and relatives. Children should not be forced to write these letters, but they should have the opportunity to do so. Some children who intend to write letters are so distracted by the many other activities that they forget about it. The rift that might exist between the child and his parent can be deepened by such negligence. Setting aside one evening a week for children to write letters when it is quiet in the unit may avoid such unnecessary conflicts. This does not prevent a child from writing more often. A child-care worker should be careful not to criticize a child for not wanting to write. This is an area which touches the very core of the child's problems and is often closely related to the reason the child is in the institution. No child should be forced or even advised to write a letter home, but he should have the opportunity to do so if he chooses. Only upon the advice of a child's caseworker or therapist should the child-care worker take any positive action in suggesting that the child write to his parents. Young children and non-readers may have to be helped to write, or may dictate to the adult what they want to say.

DARNING AND MENDING

In some units of older girls it is desirable to set a period of time aside for washing stockings and lingerie, mending, darning, and ironing. While most of the laundry and sewing needs have to be met by the sewing and laundry facilities of the institution, it is important to train adolescent girls to care for their own clothes, especially if they will soon be leaving the institution.

SUMMARY

Hours immediately after the children's return from school should not be scheduled for group activities, but should be left free for individual activity and loafing. After dinner some group activities have to be compulsory, but most should be voluntary, and should allow the child not to participate if he so chooses.

Petty Cash Fund and Allowances

Every living unit should have at its disposal a small rotating fund so the child-care worker can plan certain activities with the children which cost money. This fund should be based on the size and the age of the group, and the anticipated activities for a month. It should cover expenses for birthday parties, farewell parties, holiday celebrations, occasional special treats and possibly one additional regular event per month. The fund should also permit the worker to buy occasional knickknacks for the unit which might improve its appearance and give the children a home-like atmosphere.

Every child in the institution should have an allowance. This allowance might vary from rather small sums for younger children to appropriately larger sums for older children. Its size should be increased if the children are expected to pay for such things as haircuts, streetcar passes and toilet articles. Usually the institution provides these services without cost. The allowance should be equal for all children in each group. While children come from different backgrounds and have to be treated individually, it is wise that with regard to allowances they should be treated alike. If children receive money from home this money should be put in an account. It may only be used for their allowances and for authorized special purposes. The amount of money in a child's account should not affect the size of his allowance. Such inequality would be damaging to the rest of the children. Allowances should permit the children to buy themselves refreshments at the corner drugstore or in the institution canteen. It should cover a weekly visit to a movie if this is not provided in the institutional program itself. For older children who are permitted to smoke, it might also provide for the purchase of cigarettes, and cosmetic articles for girls. It is necessary that the children understand how the allowances are computed, but it is also important that they have the right to use their allowances according to their own judgement so long as they do not use them for destructive purposes.

Determining the allowance scale is another area in which the children can have a share. One can use the older children's interest in planning their own affairs through existing children's councils or committees formed for this purpose.

Work

Some institutions have organized work programs for children. Preparation of adolescents for employment is a very important part of their training and has already been mentioned in discussing children's chores. Work which is a regular chore expected of the child as a member of a living group should be confined to the child's unit. Work outside the living unit should be based on two alternate considerations. It must either be important for the child's vocational or rehabilitative training, or it must be paid work.

Work as part of vocational training: Children who cannot go to school on the outside and those who need additional vocational training should be offered the opportunity to prepare for a vocation in the institution. For many children this is a major advantage of their institutional stay. Delinquents in training schools often have opportunities to learn a trade at the school. Work has to be systematically coordinated in a school program which combines vocational and academic instruction. While, under certain circumstances, it could be of economic advantage for the institution, the type of work should be based solely on the vocational needs of the children. Sometimes institutions situated in rural districts drawing their clientele from urban communities overemphasize agricultural training mainly because they have farm facilities available. (The work should be based on the children's needs.) Children who have high academic capacities and interests should not be placed in a work program but in an academic one. Children who are not able to learn a complicated trade should be taught simple and uncomplicated vocations. The goal in all cases is to train the child to become independent when he leaves the institution. The childcare worker has to support the child who works and observe what the child's specific interests are so that he can help the teachers or the principal in designing a vocational program for the youngster.

Work for pay: Some institutions have found it helpful for some adolescents to work for their allowances. Only those children who are ready can do this in addition to their other functions and responsibilities. This work should not interfere with the adolescent's studies or recreational activities. Therefore, the afternoon hours after school or Saturday mornings have been found the most satisfactory periods for work assignments. The child should be paid for this work on a scale which will give him a feeling of worthwhileness and dignity though it is not comparable to a wage scale for adults. A child's work should be useful and should be evaluated by objective criteria. The decision to apply for work should be the child's, but once he has been given an assignment he should be expected to carry it out over a given period of time. The child should be paid more for this work than what he receives as his regular allowance. Usually, it is not advisable to have these children work for more than four to six hours a week. The child-care worker has to see that the child goes to his work assignment regularly, and is prepared with whatever clothing or equipment may be necessary. While he cannot be expected to supervise the child, he has to make sure that he is properly supervised in this assignment. The child-care worker should have contact with the people who supervise the youngster in his job, and should help him budget appropriately the money he receives for his work. An adolescent's work should not exclude him from the other activities of the group.

WORK OUTSIDE THE INSTITUTION

The child-care worker often discovers a youngster's readiness for work and can encourage him to apply for an outside work position. In some cases, children can find some work outside the institution on a regular pay basis. This should only be arranged for those who are approaching the time of discharge from the institution. Such a job can become an excellent transitional experience from life inside to life outside the institution.

Religious Education

The child-care worker has to identify with his institution's religious philosophy, since religious education is a very important part of the total program. In a sectarian institution the religious direction is determined by the board of directors. If the child-care worker finds himself in basic conflict with the religious philosophy of the institution, he cannot perform effectively in that setting. He has to encourage the children to identify with the religious orientation and principles of the institution by attendance at services, participation in Sunday school, and prayers at mealtimes. In a nonsectarian institution or in a sectarian institution that has children of different denominations, the child-care worker has to be able to identify with all the children. He must give each child the feeling of being protected and of belonging in spite of religious differences. The child-care worker not only must show his own respect for all faiths but must help the children to have respect for the faith of others. Some institutions have a chaplain or a person in charge of religious education who can assist individual children in planning their religious activities. The child-care worker has to identify with each child's religious pursuit without giving up his own beliefs. There must be no bias or prejudice on his part against any religious group. In nonsectarian institutions, the child-care worker has to be convinced of the basic principles of tolerance and equality.

Going to Bed

Most children, whether living in families or in institutions, resist going to bed. This resistance has many social and psychological reasons. Inertia, resentment of interruption of activities and exclusion by the adult, feelings of rejection, especially when there are other siblings who can stay up later, are only a few of these. For the child in the institution bedtime has additional hazards. For children who wet or soil or have nightmares, night is an anxiety-producing time, a time when their inner controls are least effective.

Also night poses both the wish and the fear of masturbation. Here the stimulation of the group is especially threatening.

It is not easy to make going to bed a pleasant experience. Yet much can be done for most children to make it less unpleasant than it is and to lower the child's resistance to it.

It is essential that children get an adequate amount of sleep. Since in an institution children usually have to get up somewhat earlier than in families, and since it may take them longer to fall asleep, because of the distractions of sharing the room with other children, one has to be especially careful that bedtime is sufficiently early so that children get enough sleep. Children from six to ten seem to need from ten to eleven hours of sleep each night and possibly a little nap in the afternoon; those from ten to thirteen need from nine to ten hours, and those aged from thirteen to fifteen need from eight to ten hours of sleep in an average night. The sleep needs of children fifteen years and older vary. They might increase in some cases and decrease in others. Like adults, they adjust their sleep to their needs. Bedtime should be arranged accordingly.

There are a number of do's and don't's which might be helpful in getting the children to bed more readily. No activity should be started that will extend beyond bedtime. If one permits children to watch an hour-long television show, it will take twenty more minutes before they are ready for bed. Starting a new game which cannot be finished by bedtime invites unnecessary difficulties. All outside activities should be concluded at least fifteen minutes before bedtime so the children can relax.

The last half-hour before bedtime should be a quiet period of reading, quiet games, stories, or songs. Mystery thrillers on TV or exciting comics instill fear and restlessness. The more quiet, restful, and relaxed the close of the day is, the better the chance that the children will go to bed readily and have a restful sleep. It is advisable to let the child know perhaps a few minutes before he actually has to get ready for bed that the time is approaching. Telling him that he can play for another ten minutes is a better method of getting him to go to bed than telling him that *now* he has to go to bed.

A snack before going to bed is not only a good conclusion to the day, but often necessary because children get hungry after an early supper. This snack might consist of cookies and milk, and occasionally a special surprise prepared by the child-care worker.

During this time the child-care worker is greatly needed. In the interim between getting ready for bed and going to bed a youngster will find a hundred and one things which he has to take care of "urgently"—another glass of water, something that he needs for the next morning at school, something he wants to remind the child-care worker of. What imagination and delaying techniques a single child in a family can develop! Children in institutions have an inexhaustible repertoire of delays.

Definite established routines are necessary and helpful. They should apply to all children, though flexibility is important. The routines pertain to getting undressed, washed, or showered, brushing teeth, and putting things in order for the next day. Children should have the feeling that they have completed the day's work by the time they go to bed. Putting away toys or books is a part of this. Knowing what routines are and how much time is allotted to them represents security and protection to the child. Lights should not be switched off immediately after the children get in bed. It is desirable that children, especially adolescents, have bedside lamps, so that the room lights do not disturb all the children.

NIGHT COVERAGE

A light in the hall during the night so that the children can find the bathroom easily is important for security and safety. An individual "good night" and perhaps even a good night kiss for the younger children may alleviate the feeling of loneliness and homesickness, which is often most poignant at night. Since many children are restless sleepers, get out of bed during the night, have nightmares, or are enuretic, it is important that someone whom they know is with them during the night. Where child-care workers live in the unit, as in cottage plan institutions, this is relatively easy to arrange and affords children a degree of security that is not readily attainable otherwise. Where there are night attendants it is desirable that they know the children and the children know them.

CHAPTER 5

Recreation and Play

Children usually enjoy two types of recreation: solitary activities and activities with others. In any normally developed person's daily life there is an adequate amount of time set aside for recreation. As our civilization has progressed this time has increased, so that we now spend less time working for a living and more time for leisure than past generations.

Recreation and play are especially important to children. Play is a more real part of life for children than for adults. They actually live their play. It is unreasonable to expect younger children to consider a cowboy game less real than schoolwork. Sometimes when children under twelve come home from play, they are still so absorbed in it that they need a while to find their way back to the reality of the adult world.

Recreational tastes vary widely, and what is recreation to one would be an onerous task to another. Listening to classical music might be an absorbing experience to one person, a boring chore to another.

Three requirements must be met to make an activity a recreational one: it must be enjoyable, it must be voluntary, and it must be ego-building.

The activity must be enjoyable. The person engaging in a recreational activity must find fun in it and must love to do it. Whether it is throwing a ball, playing chess, or painting a picture, the activity must always give pleasure. The choice of activity is often determined by psychological and cultural factors. It is determined by the skill and experience of a person. Many newcomers to this country learn to enjoy baseball, a game which they never knew before. Others never attempt to get acquainted with the game because their interest lies in other directions due to their personality or their associations.

The activity must be voluntary. The child must have a choice of participating or not. The most satisfying recreational activity is the one that the child chooses spontaneously. Even an activity which the child would normally enjoy can become unpleasant if he is forced into it. The child who might like to go to arts and craft, or who begs to go to the movies, will object to going, if he is sent there when he is not ready to go.

The activity must be ego-building. The child's self must feel strengthened by this recreational activity. Awareness of his skills, strength, endurance, or alertness, the feeling of being a part of a team, of having learned a new game, or of having used his intelligence successfully all contribute to increasing his self-respect and joy of living. The child should always come out of the game with more self-confidence than when he entered. Even if the child loses in a game, he may gain confidence by knowing that he can take defeat.

Every child-care worker should have a knowledge of some recreational and play activities, and should be able to participate in a number of recreational activities with the children. Perhaps it would be better to say that in every unit there should be at least one child-care worker who can participate in a number of the children's activities. Every child-care worker should be able to supervise most of the activities in which the children of his group participate, except a few where specialists are needed. If adequate supervision cannot be provided for many recreational activities the children are deprived of satisfactions necessary for their healthy growth.*

* Some books on games for the use of child-care workers ought to be available in every institution. Some of the books we can recommend are: Richard Kraus, *Play Activities for Boys and Girls 6–12: For Teachers, Parents, Recreational Workers*, New York: McGraw-Hill, 1957; Lillian and Godfrey Frankel, *101 Best Games for Teen-Agers*, New York: Sterling Publishing Co., 1951; Jessie H. Bancroft, *Games*, New York: Macmillan, 1937; Margaret E. Mulac, *Fun and Games*, New York: Harper & Brothers, 1956; Darwin A. Hindman, *Handbook of Indoor Games and Stunts*, New York: Prentice-Hall, 1955; Catherine T. Hammett and Virginia Nusselman, *The Camp Program*, New York: Association Press, 1951; and *Handy Play Party Books* (five kits), Delaware, Ohio: Cooperative Recreation Service.

Some Emotional Implications

Children engaging in games often have unconscious reasons for the choice of the game, their roles in it, and their manner of playing. It has been said already that for some children the game establishes their "own world" which is almost as real to them as the real world. More specifically, the game might be used to express anger, hostility, frustration, wishful thoughts, fantasies—all of which they cannot express in the real world. The child who selects mainly games in which he plays the aggressor might reveal as much about himself as the child who always takes the role of the victim. The child-care worker can guide the game so that frustrating experiences in the group living situation are not constantly repeated in the game. For instance, he might try to avoid a situation where the outcast of the group becomes the scapegoat in the game. Sometimes it might be healthy to let the children vent their hostility against the child-care worker which they cannot express in real life in a game.

Solitary Recreational Activities

Children in an institution should have opportunities to be by themselves, to engage in solitary activities which they enjoy. The development of the ability to keep oneself busy is as important as the ability to socialize. The child should have the capacity for both forms of recreation.

The child-care worker must know the favorite recreational activities of each child. As long as these recreational activities are not in conflict with either the law, the welfare of the other children, or the treatment goals of the particular child in question he should do everything in his power to enable the child to engage in this activity during certain periods of the day. Books should be available to children who like to read. The child-care worker can help these youngsters by arrangements with a library, by giving books as presents, and by borrowing books from others.

The child who is interested in constructive games, such as woodwork, or airplane modeling, should have the opportunity to carry out this type of activity.

When two or three children with the same interest form a relationship with each other, such activities can serve as bridges for the isolates to enter the group.

Collecting is another solitary activity. The pockets of a young boy's trousers are usually loaded with so many things that they look like a miniature junk yard. The boy wants recognition for this weird and unmethodical collection. While it is sometimes necessary to ask him to discard some of these items, such as parts of a motor, dead frogs, or pieces of glass, in general one can appreciate this collector's zest. If one takes the time to listen to these children and find out why they collected all these things, one can get real insight into their fantasies. Some of the older children collect in a more methodical way. They may collect stamps, coins, butterflies, rocks, pictures, or match covers. They organize them into intricate systems of their own, and as they grow more experienced, according to the standardized systems of collectors. They usually know the exact value of each item in their collection, and the scientific, commercial, or historic significance of their treasures. The childcare worker, in showing an interest in these activities, gives support to the children and increases their pride in their collections, as well as their confidence in themselves.

Girls can often keep busy for hours playing by themselves with their dolls and doll houses. This activity has a deep psychological meaning. The girl is creating a world for herself in which she becomes the mother and the doll is the child. Children not only recreate their own family constellation but also they express in doll play their wishes for a different, ideal family constellation. A girl who has a younger brother might create in her play a family consisting only of herself and her parents, thus indicating her basic rejection of her brother. The child-care worker can observe this, but should be careful not to interpret its meaning to the child as he might touch on deep-seated emotions. Interpretation must be left to the therapist. The child-care worker can help the child in her doll play by securing doll clothing, or improving the doll furniture. This play sometimes acts as a bridge between the individual child and another child engaged in a similar activity.

Playing with dolls is not restricted to younger girls. Many older girls would actually like to play with dolls and do so in unobserved moments. Sometimes the child-care worker has to protect such a youngster from the ridicule of other girls her age. Doll playing is not completely restricted to girls, although relatively few boys over six engage in it openly. However, with boys a stuffed animal often takes the place of a doll.

If a boy over six overtly insists on playing with dolls this may indicate that he is not proud enough to be a boy, is not completely adjusted to his sex. This should be brought to the attention of the child's therapist and must be handled according to his advice.

The child's creation of his "own world" is often an important part of solitary play. The child who is absorbed in playing with clay or mud, or by a puzzle game, the child who is so totally engulfed in building a tree house as a hide out in the woods, establishes a world for himself into which he can flee when life in the real world becomes too difficult.

Sometimes children use a doll, a stuffed animal, or some other toy as a fetish. They must have it wherever they go, especially when they need to feel safe and secure, as though they think it is invested with some magic power that can protect them. There are complex psychological reasons—all unconscious—for this attachment. The child-care worker has no choice but to respect it. He should, however, discuss it with the therapist.

For children who are restless and aggressive other individual activities are probably more common, such as bicycling, roller skating, or climbing trees. All forms of motor activity and locomotion seem to be enjoyable and relaxing to them. Children should have the opportunity for such activities. Institutional living units should include space and equipment not only to make such activities possible, but also to encourage them. Sleds, bicycles, tricycles, roller skates should, whenever possible, belong to each child. If this is not feasible they should be available in sufficient numbers in the unit so that children who enjoy these activities can engage in them freely.

For some of the more aggressive isolates a punching bag might be a good activity in which they can act out some of their aggression. All activities in which children can act out aggression without becoming destructive are desirable.

As has been stated, all these activities must not conflict with the law or rules of either the institution or the community. Therefore, bicycling in an institution in which children must remain on grounds can be permitted only within grounds. Recreational activities must not be in conflict with the welfare of the other children, and therefore must be done at a time when they do not interfere with other children's activities and in a way which cannot hurt other children. For instance, the avid reader must not delay the supper hour because he wants to finish his book. The owner of a hamster cannot use it to frighten others. The trumpet player may not practice when the children are asleep. More important, these activities must not interfere with the treatment goal for the child. If a very withdrawn child is a collector of coins and uses his coin collection in order to withdraw further from the rest of the group one might have to interfere and encourage him to participate in other activities. While supervision of solitary activities must be inconspicuous, it must exist.

Recreational Activities with Others

Many of the child's recreational activities involve other children, sometimes just one other child, sometimes the whole group. The number of children with whom a child can engage in recreational activities and the length of time in which he can enjoy such activities are one measuring rod (but only one) of the child's progress in socialization. In order to participate for any length of time with other children, certain psychological conditions must be present.

One of these is communion of interests and skills. The child who collects three-cornered hats has less chance of finding someone with the same interest than one who collects stamps. The youngster who is interested in baseball will find companions more easily than the child who is interested in fencing. The communion of interest and skills is one of the important marks of socialization.

Another condition is ability to accept rules and regulations. Even if only two children play together they must agree on certain rules for the game, and each must abide by these rules until they change their agreement. The greater the number of children who participate and the more organized an activity is, the greater is the demand on the child to submit his own interest to the rules of the group. Participation in group recreational activities, therefore means that the child can overcome his self-centeredness for a period of time and be part of a social entity. He can abandon his own need for uniqueness, and become equal with others. Disturbed children, like very young children, are often not able to participate in highly organized group activities. Their introduction into group recreation must proceed slowly, and may have to start with an adult being a partner to the activity, modifying the rules if he sees that the child's ability to submit to them has been exhausted.

The ability to compete is also necessary. Everyone participating in a group recreational activity must be able to invest himself enough so that the game is enjoyable to him and his partners. This means that the attention span of the participants must last for the duration of the game. It is a well known fact that a chess player must have a long attention span in order to play successfully. If a chess player gives up after the first six moves, his partner will possibly win an easy victory. However, he will not enjoy the game and will probably not want to play with this partner again. Similarly, a child who shows an interest in playing first base in a ball game during the first two innings, and then becomes negligent and disinterested, will not remain on the team for long. Skill and interest, therefore, must be sufficient to enable the child to become a competitor within the group. It also means that the child has to take the game seriously enough so that it represents the same challenge to him that it does to the other players. Sometimes when adults play with children they try too hard to be indulgent, and show the child that they do not really take the game seriously and, indirectly, that they do not really take him seriously. This indulgence can be degrading to some of the more alert and better adjusted children.

The ability to lose is also important. Most games have a competitive element. Losing is always hard. It suggests that one is not so good as another, and may represent a serious blow to the ego.

Nevertheless, in order to participate in any group recreational activity, one must be able to face losing. Children need preparation for the possibility of losing and may need support after they have lost. Such an experience may help them recognize that losing a game does not mean losing status nor does it reflect personal inferiority. Children who are disturbed can easily lose their self-confidence and cannot participate well in games in which they might lose.

Group recreational activities can be classified in three ways: by the degree of adult planning, by the degree of group participation, and by the degree of competitiveness.

Planning Group Activities

Many group activities are spontaneous. Children derive most satisfaction when their activities develop spontaneously. Group singing around a fireplace, or on an outing, usually starts suddenly and spontaneously. One child begins to sing, another joins in, and soon the whole group is singing. As they sing, their repertoire of songs seems inexhaustible. Neither the child-care worker nor the children themselves may have been aware that they knew so many songs.

The same might happen in telling stories or playing ball. One or two children start, and suddenly everybody seems to participate. One girl might try to set another girl's hair in an elaborate style. Others join in and soon a beauty show is in progress. These activities start with one child's taking the initiative and the others following. The principles of leadership, which were discussed before, operate in this situation.

However, spontaneity does not always work. Often after the third song there is a long silence because nobody thinks of a fourth. At that point a child interrupts by giggling, telling an unrelated story, or making an inappropriate remark, and the group activity never really gets going. At such moments the child-care worker has to participate by being ready to fill the gap when a lull in the activity occurs. His starting a fourth song might lead some other person to sing a fifth, a sixth and a seventh, rekindling the spontaneity. The child-care worker has to be sensitive and alert to the mood of the group and has to know how long such spontaneous activities should last. He has to recognize when the enthusiasm is gone, and know how to end an activity at that point.

Frequently, spontaneity can be planned for. The child-care worker has to anticipate possible group activities and be able to find occasion to introduce them in a seemingly spontaneous manner. For instance, if the child-care worker knows that Johnny has a beautiful voice, he can mention this fact to some children and make them curious and interested in Johnny's voice. Then, when the proper occasion arises and the group is in the mood for it, he can ask Johnny to sing. The chances are that immediately some of the children will support him in this request, and Johnny will feel that the child-care worker and the whole group are interested in his singing. Johnny then finds pleasure in being the focus of the group for the moment. Similarly, if the child-care worker takes his group on an overnight hike and prepares himself somewhat by refreshing his knowledge of astronomy, he can with seeming spontaneity talk to the children about the stars and the moon. This may then start a really impressive group activity of exploring the sky at night. If he has refreshed his knowledge of some card tricks he might entertain a group of children this way; if he anticipates that some children might want to fly some kites, he might take some string along, so that when the occasion arises, he is ready. He might even suggest a play to some of the children casually, so that if the discussion should happen to lead in this direction, the children will become eager to give a performance. While he knows that the children will be creative enough at times to develop spontaneous group activities, the child-care worker cannot rely on this. He helps their spontaneity a little either by preparing them inconspicuously or by preparing himself to jump into the breach if the need arises.

This is not always enough. Most group activities require more structured planning. If the group goes on a cook-out, food, charcoal, utensils and other items have to be prepared. Time of leaving, transportation, and locale have to be arranged. In structured sport activities equipment, such as uniforms, balls, and bats, is often necessary. If the group goes fishing, they need fishing rods, lines, hooks and sinkers. In the living unit itself, activities require similar preparation. If there is a party, decorations, food, and games have to be planned and prepared. A dramatic performance requires choosing a play and the cast, setting the stage, and rehearsing. So many group activities need planning ahead of time that one cannot rely solely on the spontaneity or imagination of the children. The child-care worker has to plan these things. He must, indeed, be very methodical about all the details of the activity. There are other questions he must consider. What should he do about the children who cannot participate? How much will the activity cost? How much time will it take?

With groups of younger children, the child-care worker has to make most of the plans himself. While he must inform and prepare the group for the activity, he cannot rely on their participation in the planning itself. He should know what activities the children enjoy and are ready for and allow them to help him in the preparations, but he should not delegate the planning of the activity to these children.

Group Participation in Recreational Activities

Children at different ages and with different personalities possess different degrees of readiness for participation in group activities. We have already indicated that certain solitary activities serve to bring two or three children closer together. These children, in a way, are engaged in parallel activities rather than in integrated group activities. Two children who build airplane models might do a lot of things at the same time, but only as they share tools or equipment do they really experience the satisfaction of joint constructive activity. Nevertheless, many group activities start with two or three children participating and others slowly joining in. The child-care worker has two obligations in planning group activities: to choose those in which as many children as possible might participate, and to enable as many as possible to participate in planning and preparation. Most children can participate to some degree in the activity itself. A good number of children can play a part in preparing an activity once the activity has been decided.

However, relatively few can really participate in planning. Usually the adolescent group is more able to plan on their own than the younger group. The adolescent group might not accept a group activity if they did not help plan it. An activity for adolescents quite frequently can start with setting up a planning committee. The child-care worker has to give definite instructions to such a committee so that they do not have unrealistic expectations or set unattainable goals. Often such a committee can be elected by the children. Some units have standing committees, such as student councils and cottage councils, which are charged with planning such activities. The child-care worker, in delegating the responsibilities for planning, does not relinquish his own role in it. Planning such activities is a part of the fun of the activity itself.

The same is true for the preparation of the activity. Once the group has decided on an outing much has to be done. Collecting props and camp equipment, tents, sleeping bags, fishing nets; discussing the facilities of the camp site, practicing how to pitch tents or make knots, are all important preparations for the trip. One must not make the preparation so cumbersome that the children lose their interest in the activity because of the difficulty of the preparation. Again, the child-care worker must use good judgement and be sensitive to the children's abilities and to their interest span. If each time the children want to throw a ball they have to walk a half mile to a ball field, they probably will lose some of their interest. Therefore, the child-care worker should himself participate in the preparation, especially taking over those functions which the children are either unable or unwilling to carry out.

Most children enjoy participation in the activity itself. However, they have a rather short interest span in participating in a group activity and soon someone will give up. Even in a baseball game which a child might have looked forward to for a long period of time, he might get tired after the third or fourth inning. The child-care worker has to be ready to have substitutes or to be a substitute himself so that one or two children cannot spoil a group activity in which the rest of the group have invested so much.

The Competitiveness of Recreational Activities

In a competitive society like ours, education must prepare children for the competition that they will encounter in their adult lives. Our educational system uses competition as a major method of training. We have competitive examinations in colleges, competitive sports, and a competitive system of employment. It is therefore necessary for the child to learn how to compete. On the other hand, it is equally important for each child to see himself as a worthwhile human being, to gain confidence in himself, and to see his peers as friends and supporters rather than as competitors. Only after the child has gained confidence in himself and in others is he actually ready to take part in competitive activity. Before a child is ready to engage in competitive activities, he must have a great deal of security. He must be convinced that participation and cooperation are more important than winning. Before a child is ready to participate in competitive games he must be able to enjoy these games even if he loses. Children in institutions, who often have problems about self-confidence and social integration with others, can only be introduced to competitive activities of any kind slowly. While an activity might be enjoyable for a winner, it can be depressing and ego-deflating for the loser. For each winner, there are usually several losers. Those in charge of program planning must have this dangerous aspect of competition in mind in designing a recreational program for such children.

Practically every recreational activity has competitive aspects. Any achievement that can be compared to another's achievement lends itself to creating a winner or a loser. If two children go fishing they might compare their catch in number and size. If two boys ride their bikes, they can have a race. Even children sitting around a fire singing folk songs might decide that one child sings louder or better or knows more songs than another. There are, of course, a great number of recreational activities and games, the nature of which demand that there be a winner. In a game of chess, one person has to win and the other has to lose. In a game of baseball, one team has to win and one has to lose; and a boy who hits a home run has a higher status than one who strikes out. It may well happen in a group that some children are almost always winners in sports activities, that the leaders are always unbeaten. This is quite probable because the leaders usually have a great influence in the choice of the activities and so they choose an activity in which they excel. The child-care worker, therefore, must deal with the problem of the loser. Very often his own sympathy is strongly with the losers and their resentment toward the winners. Sometimes he may actually interfere with the rules of the game in order to give the weaker and less successful participants a chance. This usually is not helpful. The child-care worker can do a number of things to help the children who do not win. First, he can find out whether there is any area in which these children can show skill. A child who might not be successful in some of the more popular group activities might have some special talents which can be used occasionally in the interests of the group, such as playing the harmonica, singing well, or having special skill in acrobatics. In a way, the child-care worker has to find in each child every possible skill which may enable him to be more acceptable and more successful. He can also try to explain before the game that winning and losing are not the major aspects of the game, but that participation is itself a gratifying experience. He can also help the children see that those who do not play the game well can learn it better, so that ultimately they too might be successful. The child-care worker can try to direct the group to a number of activities which are not so highly competitive. Sometimes he might be in a position to substitute a non-competitive game for some of the competitive ones. The recreational diet of the children has to be a balanced one and there have to be many activities in an institutional recreational program that are not competitive. Many sport activities like swimming, biking, playing ball, many outdoor activities like fishing, flying kites and hiking are not competitive in nature. The child-care worker can see to it that they do not develop into competitive games. The child-care worker can make sure that the children who are totally unable to take competition do not participate in strenuous competitive activities. If the child-care worker cannot avoid such a situation, he can help a child to recognize that he might get very angry when he loses or that he might walk out of the game in the middle of it. By anticipating this, he might avoid too much frustration for this youngster.

A Note on Television

While specific activities and games cannot be discussed in this book, we think it necessary, in view of the ever-increasing role that television plays in a child's recreational life, to add a word about it. The presence of television in most institutional living units provides the children with a pleasant, easily accessible entertainment. The feeling of being bored, not knowing what to do, can easily be remedied by turning the switch of the television set. This has certain advantages; loneliness, even the gnawing feeling of being rejected, and the inability to entertain oneself can be relieved, while at the same time an exciting and often educational world can be entered. TV can be an excellent source of entertainment for the sick child who is bedridden.

TV also has many disadvantages. It hampers a child's creative activities; it is an easy, tempting lure away from more important activities; it may slow down the child's search for companions. In group living, it may at the same time create conflicts between different children who want to tune in on different channels. Unfortunately, it also offers many programs which may well be disturbing and upsetting to children.

While the child-care worker may object to over-use of TV, it would be unwise to ban television from the institution. Instead, thought should be given to how it can be used most productively. Rules should be set up governing at what times TV is permitted, and who shall decide on the program. A democratic method of selection is necessary. Certain very popular programs may have to be standard choices. On the other hand, some programs may have to be forbidden. A clear explanation must be given in these cases. It may be more expedient to discuss such a move ahead of time. Indeed, a discussion with the children of the programs they saw, their impressions and reactions, may be helpful, stimulating and revealing.

The child-care worker should not regard the time when the

children look at television as "time off" or as time he can spend away from the children. Many times it is advisable that he see the program with the children; but even if he does not, he should be in the room, available to the children, especially to those who may not be interested in the program and want to do something different, and to those who are frightened by the program and need to feel that an adult is nearby.

Children who use television as an escape from other activities may have to be encouraged to try other forms of entertainment. This can best be done by limiting the hours in which the television set can be used.

Recreation and the Outside Community

Very often recreational activities can be used to bring the children in the institution closer to children outside it. Sometimes an institutional ball team is a member of an outside league. Children may invite outsiders for their special recreational activities, such as parties, plays, or swimming meets. As soon as children are ready to have outside contacts, such invitations should be encouraged. Similarly, recreational activities could enable the children in the institution to participate on the outside. Members of the institutional team, after they have gained skill, will join public school and other outside teams. Individual children, especially as they get ready to leave the institution, might join clubs in school and at the community center. Friends on the outside might invite them to participate in their recreational activities or family events. As children become ready for them, such activities can be important in helping them to find their way to the outside community again. Recreational activities are often an excellent bridge from the institution to the outside and help the child ultimately to adjust to life outside the institution, whether in his own home, in a foster home or in another setting.

SUMMARY

Recreational activities are a very important part of a child's life. Play is much more real to the child than to the adult. A child often cannot distinguish between the reality of his play and the reality of the rest of his life. Each child must have the opportunity to balance solitary and group recreational activities. Group recreational activities require a readiness on his part to partake in such activities. They require similarity in interests of the child, ability to submit to the rules of the game, ability to compete, and ability to lose. Competitive games, while a helpful part of a child's preparation for adult life, can only be used as the child is ready for them chronologically and emotionally. Group recreational activities vary in the degree of their spontaneity, the degree of the children's participation and the degree of competitiveness. The worker has to see to it that each child finds a successful experience in some group recreational activities.

CHAPTER 6

Discipline

In the broadest sense discipline is the "order of living." It is: the total organization of daily living; the control of one's impulses, and the willingness to submit to the tenets and commandments of the social group. In this broadest sense everything we have discussed thus far pertains to discipline. In its narrower sense discipline is more specific. Every offense disturbs the social order and violates certain rules of social living. Discipline tries to re-establish the social order and to prevent the repetition of the offense. Discipline in the broader sense is preventive in nature; in its narrower sense it is corrective.

Discipline in the Broader Sense

The child-care worker has to be sure that the order of living is clear to the children, that the children know what the tenets of the group and of society are, and what is expected of them as far as impulse control is concerned.

When a rule is broken, one must ascertain whether the rule was clear, valid and within the child's comprehension and capacity. Antiquated rules are a common ailment in institutions. There are times when controls are inadequate and must be reinforced; and other times when they should be relaxed.

Disobedience and defiance are not accidental. They often stem from impulses not within a child's conscious control. Developing the child's ego to the point where he can control his impulses is one of the major tasks of the institution. The child-care worker has to be sure that he has done his part to help a youngster in this area by conveying his understanding, interest and faith both in the child's worth and in his ability to meet established expectations.

Sometimes children commit offenses because they are confused about values and actually unable to distinguish between right and wrong. A child who sees his parents cheating on taxes, drinking, and being abusive cannot be expected to respect the values of society. Values must be set by the institution and the child-care worker must become not only the guardian of these, but also the exemplification of them in the child's eyes.

It is the obligation of the child-care worker to determine the causes of the infringements and what organizational controls or value setting processes can remedy the situation. Only after this preventive structure of discipline is established can specific correction be applied.

Discipline in the Narrower Sense

There are five different methods of applying corrective discipline. These methods are not mutually exclusive, but some of them can be applied simultaneously.

In order to pursue an effective and helpful course of disciplinary action, one must make clear exactly what the offense was, when it occurred, what provoked it, who the offenders were, and under what circumstances it took place. Johnny smashed five window panes in his cottage. Certainly he has to be called to account and possibly punished for it. However, the child-care worker found out that this offense happened on a Sunday evening when Johnny was the only one in the cottage who did not have a visitor. Johnny was especially desperate after the children came back and reported the magnificent experiences they had had on that afternoon. Through understanding its cause the offense takes on a different character; and the disciplinary action must consider the circumstances.

Every offense has to be clarified in this way, for the child-care worker, for the child involved, and very often for the other children.

Clarification alone is sometimes enough to re-establish the violated social order and to prevent the repetition of the offense. In that case no further action is needed. Ofter, however, other methods of correction have to follow.

The step after clarification is persuasion. The adult tries to persuade the individual child and/or the group to correct a mistake. The child who commits an offense often feels that he has no other way of achieving his goal. The child-care worker can show this youngster there are other ways, that he has the ability to control his impulses, that he is actually not so weak as he thinks. A child who skipped classes in school because he "couldn't stand it any longer" has no confidence in his ability to control himself. If in a discussion with the youngster, the child-care worker succeeds in increasing the child's self-confidence and in having him return to school, the situation may not need further disciplinary measures. The tone of such a discussion has to be supportive and dispassionate, emphasizing the reality consequences of the offense and how it can be corrected. The child-care worker can let the child himself suggest ways of correcting his mistakes. He can recognize whether the child has any guilt feelings about his actions and determine how these feelings affect his plans for making amends.

If one deals with a group of offenders it is wise to discuss the offense with each separately rather than with all of them, because children in a group reinforce each other's defenses of denial and defiance, and are less ready to admit their mistakes. Only after talking with each child can the child-care worker discuss with them as a group the implications of their misbehavior.

The Use of the Peer Group in Discipline

While we have emphasized the importance of group participation in almost every aspect of the daily living of children in an institution, we do not believe that the group should be used in discipline questions. The "children's jury" is destructive for the offender and for his judges. Such trials are based on the erroneous assumption that children can show objective attitudes toward the offense and the offender, and evaluate each other by the adult's code rather than by the group code. Often the children basically sympathize with the offender. Many children are punitive toward the rejected child and indulgent toward leaders. In a trial by other children, therefore, the leader finds support for his delinquent activity, while the rejected child finds himself even more rejected.

Similarly, child welfare workers should avoid group punishment if only one or two children were involved in an offense and the others really had nothing to do with it. Child-care workers become annoyed if they cannot find out who committed an offense, and are frequently tempted to use one of two methods, neither of them helpful in the long run. One, they try to act as detectives by grilling, probing, cross-examining, deducting, and inferring beyond the evidence, sometimes by threatening and frightening the innocent. The success of this method is usually very limited, and it often incurs the children's hostility toward the child-care worker rather than toward the offender. The other and more harmful method is to punish the whole group, guilty and innocent alike, in the hope that the children will betray the offender. Even if this is the result, this method is not sound, as it offends the group code and the individual's self-respect and incurs hostility against the child-care worker. Those who have been punished without cause will long remember this injustice and will use it as a confirmation of the adult's injustice and their own weakness.

Sometimes it is better to admit that one cannot find out than to find out at the expense of the child's ego. Seriously discussing the implications of the offense with the group involved is often the only thing one can do and more often the best thing one can do. A stealing episode, for example, may hurt only one child today, but may hurt the others tomorrow and certainly affects the reputation of all. In cases of offenses where safety is risked, such as firesetting, certain precautions might have to be taken which affect all children, but which should not be equated with punishment.

DISTRACTION

Distraction is a form of persuasion. Sometimes the simplest way of correcting a child is to draw his attention to some activity other than the delinquent activity in which he is engaged. This works especially well with younger children who are more easily distractible than older children. A child who throws stones at a building might be distracted to throwing a ball or engaging in some other activity.

While this form of distraction is mainly applied with children who are still engaged in the undesirable activity, another form of distraction can be used after the act has been committed—substitutional activity. The fact that boys sneak out to a girls' cottage at night may suggest that they have not enough legitimate contact with girls; such a legitimized contact might be established. Children who steal toys from other children may not have enough toys of their own. Providing toys then is a form of substituting nondelinquent activity for delinquent activity. Children who break up furniture deliberately might need a punching bag or a trampoline where they can express their aggressiveness in a socially acceptable form. Such distraction can deal with the present offense and serve to prevent future misbehavior.

INTERFERENCE

Clarification and persuasion are geared toward helping the child give up his unacceptable activity. These methods are not always sufficient. There comes a time when the adult must halt unacceptable behavior. This active interference by the adult is the next step in discipline.

The child-care worker can interfere verbally by letting a child know that he will not let him continue this behavior. In essence, he tells the child: "You cannot control yourself, but I will control·you." This gives the child the feeling that he is protected. Although at the moment he may resent the interference, he knows that somebody cares enough not to let him go on destroying his environment and ultimately himself.

Interference can be social; the child-care worker can accompany a child to prevent asocial acts. The child who has stolen from the neighborhood drugstore cannot be allowed to go there alone. The child who has disturbed another cottage can only go there in the company of an escort. This form of discipline not only shows the child that he can be protected but also that the adult does not want to eliminate his recreational pursuits but wants only to supervise him more closely.

The child-care worker can use his adult strength to restrain the child. He prevents the child from hurting another child, damaging property, or injuring himself. He may have to hold a child's hands during an outburst of destruction. He may have to put himself bodily between two fighting boys. Physical interference should be used only for protection and not for punishment.

REMOVAL

A more specific form of interference is removal of an individual from the group. This is sometimes necessary if the child's behavior tends to destroy group activity or has a damaging effect on the group. Schoolteachers often use this method to keep order in the classroom. Similarly, the child-care worker must at times remove a child to safeguard the group, as in cases of violent temper tantrums, consistent disruption of group activities, and uncontrollable physical and verbal abuse. The removal may vary in time from a few minutes to days and weeks. Whenever we remove a child from the group, whether for an hour or for a few days, into a single room within the unit or into another building, it is always necessary for an adult to be with the child. The individual child can be removed from the group but he must not be removed from the adult. During violent temper tantrums the adult might stay a sufficient distance from the child so that he cannot be bodily attacked but he must always be close enough so that the child cannot harm himself seriously. After the child has calmed down, clarification and persuasion should be used so that the child can recognize that the adult wants to help him.

RESTITUTION

In cases of property damage or theft, a realistic and simple form of discipline is restitution. The child replaces or pays for the material loss he has caused. A child who breaks a window pane pays for the window pane and for the labor involved in fixing it. A child who steals has to either return the stolen goods or pay for them. The child-care worker has to see that the child is not unduly embarrassed in the process of restitution. Sometimes, when thefts are committed, it might be wise to confront the child with the person from whom he stole. More often it is too stigmatizing for a child to be exposed as a "thief" and abandoned to the mercy of strangers. Such a procedure can seriously interfere with his rehabilitation.

Punishment

While persuasion and interference are mainly related to the immediate offense and intended to stop it, punishment goes beyond this. Punishment is intended to take place after the offense has been committed, to impress upon the offender the seriousness of his act. Punishment, therefore, is not so directly related to the offense itself as the other methods of discipline. The damage is done. The main objective of punishment is twofold: to re-establish the social and emotional order that has been disturbed by the offense, and to prevent the offender from repeating the offense. For instance, if a child hurts another child or insults the child-care worker in front of the group, the social order has been disturbed, the security and peace of the other children has been endangered. It is important for the other children to see that the child-care worker can re-establish order and peace, and can protect their security in the future. Moreover, the offender must learn that he and society can be protected from his behavior, that disturbing the order of the social group has consequences, and that adults are strong enough to provide protection.

Two basic principles should be applied to all forms of punishment: it has to be logical, and it has to be psychologically correct.

There has to be logical connection between crime and punishment. A child who refuses to get out of bed in the morning might have to go to bed an hour earlier at night. A child who does not do his chores in the morning might have to be awakened a half-hour earlier in order to do them, or he might have to miss recreational activities in the afternoon in order to make up for what he fails to do. A child who plays truant from school on Wednesday might have this considered his "day off" rather than on Sunday. He might be denied Sunday privileges.

It is not only necessary that punishment fit the crime, but that it fit the offender. If the youngster who played truant on Wednesday and has to stay in on Sunday expects a visit that day from his father whom he has not seen in a long time, it would be wrong to impose this punishment. The child might actually want the child-care worker to prohibit him from seeing his father, so that he can "get even" with his father for not having visited him regularly, or to show his father what a terrible child he is. In fact, his motivations for the offense may well lie in this area in the first place. Three boys run away together and are caught and brought back to the institution. The punishment must not necessarily be the same for all three children. One might have planned to commit burglary outside the institution, the second might have wanted to visit his mother, and the third might have run away with the others because they were the only friends he had.

Therefore, there can be no standard punishment. Punishment should be geared to logical and psychological realities. Such standard methods as deprivation of privileges, being sent to bed early, or paying a fine, are all much too simple, with the result that they do not help as punishment. In some cases, deprivation of privileges might be just the right kind of punishment; a child who has not done his homework or his chores might have to forego recreational activities; a child who steals from the drugstore might not be allowed to go to the drugstore; a child who acts up in the movies might not be allowed to attend without an adult escort. But as a general rule it is inadequate.

Some measures should be avoided because they are never logically or psychologically valid as punishment. For instance, depriving a child of seeing his parents as a form of punishment is always psychologically wrong. If there is a therapeutic reason for limiting a child's contact with his parents, this should be the determinant, not the child's behavior or misbehavior.

Physical punishment is neither logical nor psychologically correct in any case. It is seen by the child as a manifestation of the adult's aggression and of his own helplessness, rather than as punishment for his act. One might have to stop a child's acting out at times by physical interference or by removing him forcefully from the situation. This does not constitute punishment.

TIMING OF PUNISHMENT

In order to be effective and helpful, punishment should follow the offense very quickly. Delayed punishment seldom has a positive effect. Any punishment that cannot be carried out within twenty-four hours or extends over a period of time, should be discussed with the supervisor before it is imposed. In many cases the case-worker might have to be consulted as to the possible effect of such long-term punishment on the child. A child has a peculiar memory —he remembers his good deeds much better than his bad ones. Often by the time punishment takes effect, a child has already forgotten what it was all about.

When the punishment imposed by one child-care worker extends into the time on duty of another, it can cause difficulties and create conflict between the two. Such punishment is inadvisable unless one has first discussed it with the child-care worker who has to supervise it, and/or his supervisor. Sometimes it is wiser to postpone the punishment than to burden another worker with its execution.

THE CHILD-CARE WORKER'S FEELING ABOUT DISCIPLINE

In this chapter we have used the words "should," "ought to," and "must" profusely. However, in reality "musts" are not always possible. People have feelings, and where their own authority is challenged, or their control of the group threatened, their feelings direct them more than cool reason. To a certain degree this is good. It is actually the feelings of the person that count in the care of children. People who never get excited or upset about a child do not necessarily make the best child-care workers. Often child-care workers with only little understanding of the theoretical concepts of child-care have had excellent success with children, because they have warm feelings for them. The same people may get angry and annoyed, may shout and shame a child in front of others and may even slap a child occasionally. Still the totality of their interest is what helps the child, not their methods of punishment. When one is excited and has some emotional investment at stake, one does not always think of the rules or may think his method superior to that prescribed. Such emotional reactions, if they do not occur often, are natural and not necessarily damaging. It is, however, imperative that such situations be discussed immediately with the supervisor. Especially in the area of discipline, it is necessary for the child-care worker to know himself and to observe his own reactions to the children; whom he likes and whom he dislikes; to what forms of children's behavior he reacts angrily and of which he is tolerant. He has to observe, himself, whether he uses punishment as a "timesaver." Indeed punishment is very often used for that purpose. A harassed mother whose child refuses to go to bed may not have the patience to persuade him and may resort to spanking. Similarly, the child-care worker who is pressed to get his group to the dining room might be especially annoyed and strict with Johnny who delays the whole group. At this moment he might think less about Johnny's needs than about the criticism he received just recently when he brought his group to the dining room late. Thus, punishment is sometimes used because of harassment and overwork of the child-care worker himself. The old rule of the Oracle: "Know thyself!", important in all work with children, is particularly so in the areas of discipline and punishment.

SUMMARY

Discipline in the broader sense is preventive. It is the establishment of an emotional and social order for the child which prevents him from violating the rules of the social group. Discipline in the narrower sense is corrective. It is the application of various methods to correct the violation of the social order and prevent the repetition of the offense. The main methods are clarification, persuasion, interference, restitution and—only if all other methods have failed—punishment. Punishment must be logical and psychologically correct in order to be effective.

CHAPTER 7

Parents

The child-care worker not only has contact with the children but, in many institutions, also with the parents. While in some institutions parents do not visit directly in the living quarters of the children, in many others they do. Even if the child-care worker does not have contact with the parents personally, he must know about the parents in order to be able to understand the child's reaction to them.

Parents whose children need institutional care have had many experiences that threatened their security and happiness, often dating back to their own childhoods. Death, sickness, divorce and separation may have disrupted their own early lives. The advent of the child may have increased their insecurity rather than bringing new happiness into their lives. Conflict within their own family and social group, economic and professional insecurity, may have filled their lives with disappointment. They are too preoccupied with their own feelings, their own struggle for life, to give the children the attention they need. Parenthood becomes especially difficult if a child has any physical or intellectual handicap, or if he gets involved in activities which the parents do not understand or cannot control.

Society usually has a punitive attitude toward parents. While it has more or less stopped branding maladjusted children as "bad" and tries to understand children's behavior, society has not yet developed as understanding an attitude toward parents. Very often parents are blamed for the misfortunes of their children and therefore have to carry not only the burden of their own unhappiness and of their children's problems, but also the stigma of being considered "bad parents." If somebody had stretched out a hand to these weak and unhappy people when they were young and given them the help that society today tries to give to their children, undoubtedly many of them would have made good parents.

Some children have to be protected from the destructive activities of their parents. However, one must not underestimate the importance of parents to their children even when the children may have to be removed from their homes. Visiting, mail and gifts may have to be more controlled, but in most cases they should be allowed.

In a modern institution, a number of children have parents whose lives were not so bleak and upsetting as those mentioned above. Children in some of the residential treatment centers have emotional disturbances that cannot be easily explained on the basis of the parents' problems. Often the parents seem to have done everything that any good parent would do; nevertheless, disturbances develop in the child. Nobody can say exactly why. In recent years, when the problem of delinquency was no longer confined to the lower economic group but involved children of the middle class and the professional group, people began to ask what happened. Sometimes one has to go back to seemingly irrelevant experiences in the child's life or in the parents' lives to find causes for the child's behavior.

Society especially frowns upon parents who place their children away from their own homes, in foster homes or institutions. In reality, many of these parents show a greater concern than those who keep their children at home. Some have recognized they are not able to give their child the care and guidance he needs, or that the child needs special help. They deserve approval rather than disapproval when they get needed help. In the last few years, the child welfare field has begun to recognize this and to develop a more appropriate approach to parents.

Parents need help to understand that they are still parents, in spite of the child's placement. Child-care workers must always remember the adage that one can take children away from parents but one cannot take parents away from children. No other relationship that a child makes during the rest of his life can really substitute for his relationship and his feelings for his own parents.

Therefore, in order to help a child, one has to help his parents act as parents to him to the best of their ability.

Parents must know when they can visit and where, what the mail and gift regulations are, how they can participate on special occasions such as birthdays and holidays. This is the beginning of helping the parents to take the child back.

While some children cannot go back to their own homes but have to be placed in a foster home after their stay in the institution, most children do go home.

THE CHILD-CARE WORKER AND THE PARENTS

Most of the work with parents has to be done by skilled, professionally trained workers. Aside from the lack of special training, child-care workers are particularly handicapped in contacts with parents. Parents see child-care workers as rivals who remind them conspicuously of their own failure as parents.

> Mrs. Jones could not take care of her son, Jimmy, but sees that Mrs. Smith, the child-care worker, can take care of him. Mrs. Jones has feelings about Mrs. Smith. She may not show any anger openly. She may even express her gratitude to Mrs. Smith for giving good care to her child. Nevertheless, inside she may feel depressed and angry about her own inadequacy as a mother.

When parents meet a child-care worker, they may be either very ingratiating or very demanding. Nevertheless, frequently they try to show the child-care worker that he is not so perfect either. They may find the living room disorderly, the tablecloth torn, the floor dirty, and they become unduly upset about it, even though they may be poor housekeepers themselves. These observations permit them to criticize the institution and to hide their own feelings of inferiority.

> Mrs. McIntyre was constantly criticizing the institution, especially its clothing arrangements. She complained that Johnny had been promised new clothing but had received hand-me-downs. Although Johnny had relatively good clothing, she insisted that he was dressed like a "bum." She complained to the child-care worker, to the supervisor, to the director and even wrote to the board president. Finally, at

Easter time, along with everybody else, Johnny got a complete new outfit. At that time the adolescents had a fad of wearing white shoelaces in black shoes. When Mrs. McIntyre came to visit her son, he was dressed in his new outfit. She looked him up and down, examining his new attire without saying a word. Finally, she saw the white shoelaces and remarked: "This is the kind of shoelaces they give you at this place?"

Mrs. McIntyre was probably somewhat unhappy that her son now had such nice clothes. It meant to her that the institution was the good parent rather than she. The shoelaces signified that the institution was not perfect after all.

The child-care worker should keep himself informed through the caseworker about the nature of the child-parent relationship, what the specific problems of the parents are, and what his approach to them should be. This information will help him to understand the child better, to distinguish between reality and fantasy in the child's discussion of his parents, and to enable them both to establish the best relationship to each other while the child is in the institution. The child-care worker must know how to handle telephone calls, messages, mail and gifts, from the parents to the child. It is especially important that he play a constructive part with regard to vacations and visits.

Child-care workers should make parents feel at ease and treat them as welcome guests. When parents question the child-care worker's functioning in the operation of the unit, instead of becoming defensive he should try to explain why things are done this way. If something is really wrong, the child-care worker had best admit it and assure the parents that the mistake will be corrected. It does not help to try to combat the parents' attitude toward the institution. While the child-care worker must refer parents with questions concerning their children to the social worker, there are questions which the child-care worker cannot refuse to answer without giving the impression of being impolite or evasive.

Usually, it is wise to accentuate the positive experiences. If the child has made progress in school, the child-care worker may indicate this. If he has not done well but has made efforts, this can be pointed out; and if he has not made any progress, the child-care worker may say: "Well, I have not observed much change yet, but I think the social worker will be able to discuss this with you more fully."

Parents often are a little lost during visiting hours. After the first greetings are over and the important questions asked, they do not know what to do with the child. Go to a movie? Walk around the grounds? Go to the neighborhood drugstore? The neighborhood may be strange and isolated. The child may have been to the drugstore only yesterday. He may want to avoid talking with his parents by asking them to take him to the movies. Suggestions on what to do may be welcome. The child-care worker may know how the child would enjoy spending time with his parents. Perhaps a game of table tennis with a visiting father, a trip to the zoo, a game of chess. Doing things which they can enjoy together is important. For this reason movies do not seem to be the most desirable joint activity. Suggestions should be offered, preferably when they are requested, lest parents think that the child-care worker wants to "run" their lives as he runs the life of their child.

The child-care worker should refrain from getting into any specific discussion with a parent about a youngster. Anything the child-care worker says can be misinterpreted. A remark that the child made a good adjustment might mean to the parent that the child is ready to come home or that the institution threatens to send him home. If the worker says that the child is making a poor adjustment, the parent might interpret this to mean that the institution does not know how to take care of the child, or that the child is "bad." The child-care worker should try not to get involved with the parents, personally or professionally. He should refer them to the appropriate social worker.

After a child has visited with his parents he is usually somewhat upset. Even if the visit went well, the separation from the parents may be disturbing. The child-care worker must be aware of the child's mood and sensitive to his reaction after a visit with his parents. These reactions may show themselves in temper outbursts, mild depressions, provocative behavior or withdrawal. Observation of these reactions is important also for the caseworker. The child-care worker should keep the caseworker informed about the reactions of the child before, during and after the parents' visit. After a visit with parents, the child-care worker should not immediately remind the child that he did not make his bed right in the morning, or that he forgot to empty the wastepaper basket. On the other hand, he should not be oversolicitous of the child, either. The best approach is one of casual friendliness and readiness—if needed —to sympathize with the child's renewed separation pains.

The child-care worker should not discuss parents with the child. Children are sensitive about this; even if they criticize their parents severely, they resent adults doing it. The child-care worker should listen to the child's feelings about his parents but he must not give the child his own opinion of his parents. Even if the child agrees with him at the time, he may later resent any remark about the parents which could be interpreted as disparaging.

SUMMARY

Work with parents as well as with children has to be based on understanding that they are unhappy people and need help. In all cases, the underlying principle must be that parents are the guardians of the child. While parents cannot temporarily fulfill all their parental functions, they should be enabled to fulfill as many as possible, while the child is at the institution, and be prepared to assume their total parental role as soon as the child returns home again. The amount of work with parents, the intensity of the contacts, the visiting and vacation arrangements, all depend on the readiness of the parents and the readiness of the child. Therefore, planning with the parents should be the responsibility of the professional staff, while the child-care worker extends hospitality to them, consistent with the child's and the parents' needs.

CHAPTER 8

The Child-Care Worker Is Part of a Team

General Concepts

The child-care worker shares the child with many other people in the institution. He does not work alone but as a member of a staff where each has a role to play in the child's life. The better he knows what his own function is and how it distinguishes itself from the function of the others, the more helpful he can be. Along with the understanding of his role with the children, it is his awareness of being a part of a team which enables him to turn for advice and help with problems on the job. Thus, caseworkers, group workers, supervisors, psychiatrists, teachers, maintenance personnel and volunteers can be of specific help to the child-care worker and he can be of assistance to them.

It is good to remember that teamwork is necessary for the education of all children, even those living in their own homes. No child is raised by his parents alone. From the moment the umbilical cord is severed, other people participate in determining the course of a child's life. The father shares in the physical and emotional care of the child. The doctor, the nurse, the clergyman, other relatives, all begin to play a role and help the mother in nurturing the child. Later, nursery school, kindergarten and public school teachers, principals, summer camp directors, counselors and the child's peers all participate in the child's upbringing. Only as the parents are able to utilize successfully all these "team members" is the child's education successful. This team which serves the child in his own family is not planfully put together but develops gradually.

In an institution, the team responsible for the child's education should be planfully organized and selected. The child-care worker is a member of the team, but he is not the only educator. No one can play the game alone. Everyone in the institution is an educator; everyone's capacities have to be used to the fullest extent to bring about the successful re-education of the child.

For the new child-care worker who comes to an institution, the job of knowing who is who among the staff may be more complicated than the job of knowing the children. In the larger institution especially, the number of personnel, their status, their function, their interaction may seem overwhelming. The child-care worker may ask himself, "Where do I fit in? How can I ever play a part in all that?" The quicker he sees organization in this complexity of people the sooner will he be able to find his own way in the institutional maze. Only after this has been achieved can he really participate in teamwork.*

While clear organization makes it easier for the child-care worker to find his way within the team, a basic personal attitude on the part of everybody is necessary in order to achieve this teamwork. First, this involves respect for the other worker. The child-care worker has to be convinced that not only his own job, but also everybody else's, is important. While he might not be able to understand the details of the other staff members' work, he must assume that it is essential to the total function of the institution. Beyond that, he has to give other staff members credit for wanting to do a good job. He has to have faith in his colleagues' good intentions even if he is dissatisfied with their performance. He must be able to expect the same attitude toward his work. Second, interest in the work of the other people is another personal attribute which makes teamwork easier.

The maintenance man who repaired a chair yesterday which

---

* The administration can facilitate this process by a number of measures which enable the child-care worker to see his own and the others' functions more clearly:
  1. a clear job definition at the time of hiring, which outlines as exactly as possible the major aspects of the work;
  2. a written employment practice code which stipulates the rights and duties of all employees, such as work week, salary ranges, vacation and sick leave privileges;
  3. a clear definition of the lines of authority;
  4. a clear system of communication between staff so that all people involved know as quickly as possible the experiences of the children, and can participate in planning for them.

broke down again today suspects that the child-care worker was not supervising the children adequately. He does not know of the trouble the child-care worker had preventing the children from breaking up the rest of the furniture. The child-care worker, on the other hand, might not have given any thought to the maintenance man's feeling of frustration when he sees his handiwork of yesterday destroyed today.

It is usually easy to criticize others, but it is hard to criticize oneself constructively, without self-debasement and a sense of defeat. In a team it is necessary that each one ask himself, "What did I do to bring about a breakdown in teamwork, and what can I do to make the teamwork better?" This requires a good deal of honesty with oneself. Only one who is able to criticize himself is entitled to criticize others.

While the child-care worker cannot do the psychiatrist's job and the psychiatrist cannot take on the teacher's duties, and so forth, it is necessary that, if need arises, each is willing to pinch-hit to the degree that his function and knowledge permits. Someone gets sick, a child is suddenly indisposed and needs special attention, the heating system does not work, transportation arrangements break down—all these contingencies require readiness to help and to substitute for one another. The child-care worker who was delayed on his way to work must know that someone will take his place until he arrives. He can feel this more readily and justifiably if he had done unto others as he expects them to do unto him. If the maid could not come one morning, or the coach had to miss a game, the child-care worker might pinch-hit.

There is dignity to any work, especially if it is done in the interest of the children. This does not mean that day after day the child-care worker should have to take on someone else's tasks, for then he could not carry out his own.

This readiness should include helpfulness to a person new to the institution. There are so many rules and regulations to learn and people to meet, that the new worker can be confused, and often feel helpless. Children are inclined to take advantage of a new person and of his ignorance of regulations and procedures. The senior staff members have a responsibility to help a new colleague. They can unobtrusively assist him to understand his job and achieve satisfactory performance. The supervisor alone cannot do it. Often in the first few days, the personal friendliness shown a new staff member by his colleagues is more effective than any other professional help.

Because people who work in institutions often reside there, they are not only co-workers but neighbors. Like any group, they are good neighbors if they are ready to assist each other to make their personal lives as pleasant as possible. They advise each other on the shopping facilities in town, share rides in their cars, perhaps go to the movies together, or just get together and talk. The feeling of having people around who are ready to assist the child-care worker socially gives a feeling of personal and social well-being, which is an important condition to the satisfactory performance of his job.

Inter-Staff Communication

The child-care worker must feel that he has a part in plans and decisions. Regular and spontaneous contacts between the child-care worker and the other staff, joint meetings of all the staff involved are necessary implements to smooth interaction.

The child-care worker's job is a twenty-four-hour one. Even if he works only eight hours, he must know what happens to the child at all times. Communication between him and all others who deal with the child is imperative. Some of the contacts can be indirect, through the supervisors, caseworkers, or group workers who may serve as liaison between the child-care worker and the school, the special recreational counselors, or the clergyman. In all cases, however, the exchange of knowledge and experience has to flow smoothly, and the child-care worker must be sure that information given or received from an intermediary is transmitted promptly and correctly. Generally contacts between the child-care worker, the caseworker and the teachers have to be direct and personal.

Appointments should be kept on time. Disregard for the other person's time is disregard for the importance of his work. While emergencies may cause delay, in general appointments should be kept on time.

Teamwork means that the value of contacts is not unilateral but mutual. If the members of one group feel that they are the "teachers" of the other group of staff, the productivity of their collaboration is questionable. In an institution everyone can learn from everyone else. To be sure, there are specialists who know more in certain areas than others do. The caseworker or the psychiatrist, for instance, is expected to know more about dynamics of child behavior, about the causes of a child's problems, than the child-care worker. The child-care worker knows more about the child's adjustment in the group, about his everyday reactions to people and events, than the caseworker. Teachers and recreational workers contribute to understanding and to the progress of the child. Yet staff contacts are fruitful only if all members recognize each other's special competence.

Differences of opinion are to be expected and are healthy. The democratic team approach presupposes the ability and right of each participant to present his own ideas and observations, and to give consideration to the ideas of others. Out of these different ideas a joint plan evolves. It is difficult to implement a plan with which one disagrees, yet this is necessary at times, and the child-care worker is expected to do so in a convincing way. To do otherwise would confuse the child. The attitude and reactions with which a plan is put into effect should not betray to the child the differences of opinion which may have existed.

COOPERATION OF CHILD-CARE WORKER AND OTHER STAFF MEMBERS

One cannot work twenty-four hours a day, seven days a week, fifty-two weeks a year. Every child-care worker, therefore, must at times be relieved. Furthermore, because of the size of the group and the needs of the children, it may be necessary to have more than one child-care worker with the group at the same time. Since they share the child's life almost as parents do in a family, the relationship between child-care workers in the same group must be a good one. Children who come to the institution from their own homes have seen competitiveness and conflict between the adults important in their lives. They need to see that adults can work together cheerfully and without strife and conflict. Children may use any conflicts between adults for personal gain or to assure themselves that their parents were no exception. Frequently, therefore, they play one adult against the other. Whatever the immediate gain, however, it is at the expense of inner security and stability. Child-care workers must, at all times, be aware of this, lest they increase the child's problems.

All child-care workers in a unit must feel that the work is divided fairly and that their assignments have been clearly and wisely distributed. At the same time, they must be assured that their own particular skills have been utilized. If there is only one child-care worker in a unit he has to try to the best of his ability to fulfill the demands made upon him. This is a very difficult task because the functions of the child-care worker are so manifold, that it is impossible to be equally skilled in all the aspects. If there is more than one child-care worker in a unit the job can be more selectively divided. The better athlete may be in charge of the sport activities. The better housekeeper may supervise the children's clothing, etc. By utilizing and giving credit to each other's best qualities child-care workers can help each other to accept also their weaknesses.

COOPERATION

Every child-care worker must share with his co-workers knowledge, responsibilities and work materials. If one child-care worker has to attend a conference about a child he should discuss with the others the thinking and decisions evolved. A stimulating lecture, a thought-provoking book, or a child's amusing remark—all are worth sharing. It is particularly important to share work materials such as keys, funds, clothing, requisition blanks, the combination of the mailbox and the list of dental appointments. If allowances are to be distributed on Saturday morning and the funds were not left for the relief child-care worker, unhappy reactions may be expected from the children. Child-care workers must spend time with each other to discuss common problems and joint tasks. While in their work together many opportunities will arise when they can discuss things informally, it is desirable to schedule ten or fifteen minutes a day for child-care workers of the same unit to confer. It is especially important that child-care workers meet with people who relieve them before the relief period starts and again after it ends. Some communication can be in writing. Thus notes about appointments, schedules and programs may be left by the outgoing worker for the incoming one. Child-care workers who are on duty at the same time have to meet to divide such functions as who will take one group of children to the movies, who supervises the morning bathroom routines, who the breakfast preparation. Cooperation in larger areas of the work can break down if cooperation in details is not achieved.

The relief child-care worker has a very difficult assignment. He may have excellent ideas about how to do things and he may disagree with the work of the regular child-care worker. Essentially, however, the best relief job is done by those who can carry on in the spirit of the regular child-care worker. Thus, it is not helpful for the relief to relax the rules or to try to establish greater discipline during his two days of duty. The security which the children need lies in the continuation of the climate which has been established in the unit.

FRICTIONS

Child-care workers are human and at times angry feelings arise between them. These feelings, often of rivalry and hostility, are real and understandable. One child-care worker may have a greater appeal to some child than another, may have recreational skills which endear him particularly to some children, may be a fluent talker and "steal the show" from another in conferences. One may feel that his associate does not carry his share of the work, or that the administration appreciates his colleague more than him—there are many possible causes for feelings of rivalry. Even the fact that people do not like each other's personal traits, political opinions or favorite baseball clubs can lead to frictions.

Once angry feelings exist, they cannot be denied but should be faced. Some conflicts can be avoided by talking about them before occasional criticism accumulates into permanent bitterness. Some of these feelings must be discussed with the supervisor. A re-arrangement of schedule or a discussion of functions and concepts may be necessary. Sometimes those who have been with the institution for many years resent the new, young people who seemingly have the administration's confidence. In such a case, the child-care worker has to ask himself whether his resentment of his associate is not actually a resentment of the administration's new child-care philosophy and its changed policies. In that case, he has to examine whether he understands this new philosophy and how he can adjust to the new policies. This should be openly discussed with the supervisor before bitterness and insecurity impair the child-care worker's efficiency.

The Child-Care Worker and the Supervisor

The child-care worker has a big and complicated job. To whom shall he turn if he needs advice and guidance, support and direction? To which of the many "experts" in the institution should he be directly responsible? To whom should he go when he is dissatisfied with his job, when things seem overwhelming and frustrating? To whom should he bring new ideas and suggestions? Who should evaluate his work? We have referred several times to the supervisor of the child-care worker. While the caseworker, the administrator, the group worker, the teacher, and the psychiatrist may play a helpful and constructive role in the child-care worker's many functions, it is the supervisor's task to help him develop the necessary skills, qualifications, attitudes and satisfactions. He should know that there is one person, to whom he is directly responsible—the supervisor who helps him do a job which is satisfactory to the institution and to himself.

Every day the new child-care worker discovers new facets of his job. Some of these are unpredictable, but most of them can be anticipated. A sudden premature cold wave might be unpredictable,* but a seasonal one can be planned for. Which one of the many tasks comes first? What has priority over what? No

* See Appendix.

one can do everything that has to be done at once. Only as a child-care worker understands the total job can he assess priorities and organize the many tasks. Only then does the overwhelming multiplicity of chores lose its threatening and confusing aspect. The child-care worker has to be able to turn to the supervisor for help in this organization so that he can distinguish securely between the desirable, the long-range and the immediate.

Sometimes the most immediate events are so much on our mind that we forget the long-range view. A child's temper outburst at lunchtime might let us forget his good adjustment during the past week. A child's sudden delinquent activities might impair our perspective of his total progress. The child-care worker, who lives with the children and has to deal with their current behavior, sometimes needs help in looking back over a period of time and seeing this behavior in the light of the child's past progress. The supervisor can enable the child-care worker to develop such a perspective.

An institution is a breeding place for emergencies. Not only because in work with children situations always occur which demand immediate attention, but also because of the complexity of the organization itself. A leaking faucet, a delay in the laundry delivery, the absence of a cook, a short circuit in the electricity, all can create emergencies which interfere with the planned program. Sometimes a whole day's activities seem like one uninterrupted series of emergencies. The child-care worker feels exhausted, the children feel tense and "on edge" on such a day. The child-care worker may ask himself which of these emergencies were really "emergent," and which could have been avoided. Again, the supervisor can help him recognize and master the real emergencies, and relieve him of some of the tensions they bring about.

SUPERVISORY RELATIONSHIP

The child-care worker often may ask himself, "How am I doing?" "Could I have done differently?" "Was my decision the right one?" "Why do I like John better than Jay?" "Why do I have more difficulty in maintaining order than my co-worker?" "Why does Mike always seem to be angry with me?" "How can I help Clarence to do his homework?" These and many other questions come up during a day's work. Some of these might be critical of other staff members, and some might be self-critical. The child-care worker should be able to discuss these questions with the supervisor freely and openly. Indeed, the supervisor can be of help only if the worker shares freely with him his experiences and reactions.

While the supervisor gets some information about the group living unit from his own observations and from conferences with other staff members, by far the most important source of information is the child-care worker himself. An atmosphere of frankness and confidence between the child-care worker and the supervisor is essential. If the supervisor has received complaints about the dirtiness of the unit and he asks the child-care worker, "Do you think your unit is clean?", the child-care worker must be able to answer, "No, I don't," if he really thinks it is not. He may give reasons why this is so. The maid service was not good enough, the children do not participate in the work enough. This gives the supervisor not only the facts as the child-care worker sees them, but also his attitude toward them and his activities.

If the child-care worker reports to his supervisor, the latter is in a better position to help him. When, for example, the child-care worker reports, "Johnny is unhappy. He does not participate. He dislikes me in particular. What can I do?", he gives the supervisor useful information. He can find out what part of the day Johnny seems most unhappy, how he expresses his unhappiness, how his dislike for the child-care worker is shown, how the other children react to it. This information then becomes important to the supervisor's understanding of Johnny, of the group, and of the child-care worker's job. Only with frank reports from the child-care worker can the reports of other staff and his own observation be useful to the supervisor. In order to get help from the supervisor the child-care worker must have a relationship with him which permits this frankness.

He must feel free to admit mistakes, knowing that every mistake to which he admits will not be held against him, but rather will be used as a starting point in his learning how to avoid repeating it.

Written Reports

In some institutions the child-care workers keep written records, which generally consist of reports on individual children or on group activities. Sometimes records are kept in diary form. Other institutions have established check list reports. The child-care worker notes certain items, such as the number and kind of activities in which a child participated and the degree of his participation. Some of these reports contain vital statistics on such matters as a child's health, school attendance, and number of visitors. While descriptive reports may be preferable to the check list, all forms aid the child-care worker in the process of learning. The very fact that he has to sit down to review a month's, a week's, or a day's work gives him the opportunity to evaluate his performance, and to compare it with another month, week, or day. Looking at oneself is an important condition of learning about work with children. Written reports give one a view of all the events of a period rather than a few.

Unfortunately, not many institutions allow the child-care worker time to prepare written reports. Some child-care workers have only a limited interest in writing reports or filling out check lists. Both these factors have delayed the development of written reports in this field.

EVALUATION

Written reports and oral reports used in the supervisory conference should help the child-care worker to see where he stands in terms of his own expectations and those of the institution. Some conferences should be set aside especially for evaluating the child-care worker's performance over a period of time. Evaluation conferences should be held within the first six months of his employment and at least yearly thereafter. They should cover the child-care worker's relationship to the child, his ability to work with groups, to manage and organize the unit, to work with other staff, to use supervision, and to fit into the administrative structure and function of the agency. They should help the child-care worker see his strengths and weaknesses, his progress and where he needs to improve. They should indicate the degree of the child-care worker's personal investment in his job and his willingness and ability to learn.

SUMMARY

The importance of supervision cannot be overestimated. The supervisor is a teacher from whom the child-care worker learns the facets and organization of his job and through whose guidance he attains greater competence. He is the advocate of the child-care worker who helps him with the stresses and responsibilities of his job. He is the link to the administration and to the institution, who helps the child-care worker understand and fulfill his assigned functions as part of a team.*

The Child-Care Worker and the Caseworker (Therapist †)

Among the many staff members with whom the child-care worker has contact, the caseworker has a special place. Because of his intimate knowledge of the child and his close contact with him and his parents, a close working relationship between the caseworker and the child-care worker is very important.

Any child who lives in an institution is there for a purpose. To achieve the purpose of institutionalization, certain changes are necessary within the child and within his environment. In cases where the major reason for the child's placement stems from his environment, the changes within the child are less vital than the changes within the environment. In cases where his own problems are the reason, the main changes have to occur within the child.

* In view of the importance of the supervisory conference, we will give an example of a supervisory conference as an appendix.

† Since most institutions have caseworkers we use the term "caseworker" in this discussion for all professional staff who have direct treatment contact with the child. In some institutions, this is done by psychiatrists and/or psychologists. Yet, even in the latter cases the contact between the therapist and the child-care worker is often maintained through the caseworker.

In most institutions it is the caseworker's responsibility to watch that the changes within the child and within his environment are effected so that the child can be discharged at the earliest possible time.

While everybody in the institution is an important part of the treatment team, it is the caseworker (therapist) most specifically who provides the child and his parents with the opportunities for change.

The caseworker works with the child in three main areas: (1) He helps him accept his present reality situation. The child has to cope with his feelings about being separated from his parents and about living in an institutional environment and has to submit to rules and regulations to which he was not exposed in his own home. He needs help to make the best use of all the facilities in the institution. (2) The caseworker helps the child to find out what in his past experiences has contributed to making him the person he is. He may help him to trace his feelings of anger, depression, defiance and jealousy back to intimate experiences in earlier years. (3) The caseworker helps the child to plan for the future, to see realistically whether he can return to his own home or must go to a foster home, and what the prospects for his success in school are.

In order to achieve these goals, the caseworker must have a very special relationship with the child. The child must have confidence in his caseworker and feel free to talk with him about all his feelings, even the negative feelings he may have against the caseworker. For some children who are in intensive treatment three or four times a week, this relationship becomes so important that any other one seems at times irrelevant. In order to achieve this relationship the child has to feel sure that the caseworker will not use what he tells him against him, will not get angry with him for anything he says, and will keep their discussions in strict confidence.

How to be a confidant and at the same time a teammate is indeed a complex question. The caseworker certainly is interested in having the child behave well, abide by the rules of society, such as school attendance. On the other hand, if he shows too much interest in the child's social conformity, the child will make himself inaccessible to treatment.

While the child-care worker also has to have a good relationship with the child, the focus is the child's behavior in the immediate situation. The relationship between the caseworker and the child is therefore different from that of the child-care worker and the child. This difference affects the relationship between the child-care worker and the caseworker.

Sometimes child-care workers feel that caseworkers do not support the child-care worker's attempts to help the child behave; they might even feel that the caseworker supports the child's behavior. This is not so, generally. The caseworker, like the child-care worker and the teacher, wants to help the child to behave well ultimately. But the caseworker's method, one of free and uninhibited discussion, makes it impossible for him to interfere with the child's behavior; he has to leave that role to others on the staff. To bring about and maintain the confidential relationship necessary to help the child with his inner problems requires close cooperation between the child-care worker and the caseworker. Perhaps no other inter-staff relationship is so crucial to the child. Both have to understand what is wrong with the child, the purpose of his stay at the institution, the goals for him, and how they can be achieved. They have to agree on the role each one has to play in order to achieve these goals.

It is therefore necessary that the caseworker and the child-care worker discuss the child's development frequently even before the child arrives. The child-care worker has to know about the child's problems, the youngster's background, and his past experiences that might affect his present reactions. (See Chapter 1, page 11.) The child-care worker can get much of this information from the caseworker; in some cases he can get it from his supervisor. From here on, there must be give-and-take between the child-care worker and the caseworker.

The caseworker has to rely on the child-care worker's ability to observe and report the significant behavior of the child. The child-care worker has to rely on the caseworker's ability to interpret the behavior and its meaning in the daily life of the child. For example, he will certainly treat aggressive, defiant behavior differently if he knows that the child is deeply worried about his parents' impending divorce or about his father's alcoholism. He has to rely on the caseworker's willingness to share with him plans for the child such as visits, vacations, school changes and ultimately, discharge.

Child-care workers should feel that they are participating in planning for the child rather than that they are merely "told," sometimes even by the child himself. Child-care workers and caseworkers are colleagues. They are equally important in the total treatment of the child. Sometimes frictions may arise just because of this basic equality. The child-care worker may feel that the caseworker does not appreciate the difficulties of the child-care worker's job, that he sees only the individual child but not the group, that he is too theoretical, too demanding, too aloof. Usually, such frictions are based on a lack of knowledge of each other's work and can be straightened out through better acquaintance and longer experience with each other.

Conflicts always arise between people who work in such a difficult and precarious area, where success is so unpredictable. The accumulation of feelings of resentment and friction can only be a handicap. If the child-care worker has a complaint against the caseworker, he should discuss it with his supervisor, and afterwards possibly with the caseworker directly.

SUMMARY

Together with the child-care worker, the caseworker plays a crucial role in the child's rehabilitation. They share the child in a most intimate sense. While each is in a different relationship with the child, both are equally important. Through regular contacts between them, an understanding of the child and his treatment progress will be promoted and the respect for each other's part in helping the child will increase.

The Child-Care Worker and the Teacher

Next to the caseworker and the child-care worker, the teacher is most essential to direct work with the child. In many institutions the child-care worker has little direct contact with the teacher, since this is usually the caseworker's responsibility. In all institutions the child-care worker has to be aware of the teacher's role with the child, and the teacher must be familiar with the child-care worker's job. Often this information is transmitted through a third person. The child-care worker must know in what areas a child excels in school, and in what areas he is deficient, what his behavior in school is like and how he himself can work with the teachers to help the child improve. The child-care worker, whenever feasible, should be a member of the PTA group and attend their meetings whenever possible. He should get to know the teachers, and invite them to the living unit at times so that they can see how the child lives. In order for a teacher to be most helpful to a youngster, he has to understand the difference between living in an institution and living in a family.

In an institution with its own school, the relationship between the child-care workers and the teachers can be much more easily established. Joint get-togethers are possible and necessary. The teacher's participation in the child's life and child-care worker's participation in the child's education are very important parts of the total education and treatment of the child. In institutions where child-care workers have direct responsibility for all contacts with teachers, the child-care worker and the teacher should hold discussions at regular intervals, at least once a semester. As in any other relationship, mutual understanding between the people who work directly with a child is valuable and important. If they approach each other with a desire to understand each other and to help the child succeed in the areas in which each works, a good relationship will develop readily.

A child-care worker should know what the homework arrangements are. If he knows that a youngster has to prepare for math every Tuesday and for French every Wednesday, he can help this child fulfill this obligation. Similarly, if the teacher knows the child-care worker and has confidence in him, she will assume that the child-care worker was not negligent when a youngster arrives at school dirty and disheveled. If she does not know the child-care worker she may well have doubts about his standards. (See note, also, under section on homework, on getting the children off to school and on after school routine, Chapter 4.)

The Child-Care Worker and the Administration

The child-care worker, like any other staff member, is ultimately responsible to the head of the institution, the administrator. He has, therefore, to know what the administrator's main functions are and through what channels he can have access to him.

The administrator of the institution is the one person who is ultimately responsible for everything that happens to the child, in his cottage, in the casework program, in his recreational life, his health or in his education. As far as the board and the community are concerned he is in charge of the institution. They vest in him the authority and the responsibility to set up a program whereby children can be helped in accordance with the stated purpose of the institution. He represents the institution to the outside and organizes it. Although he delegates a number of these responsibilities to others, at no time can he delegate the ultimate responsibility for the total program.

In the last analysis, the administrator's responsibility is not only to determine the structure of the program of the institution but also to set the tone of the institution, the mode of interaction between adults and children, the "climate" as it has been called. Whether this tone is one of freedom or suppression, of stiffness or ease, depends vastly on the administrator's own attitude. The child-care worker, however, has to be ready to help the administrator to fulfill his function. He must know that, in making decisions, the administrator has to consider many aspects, not just the interests of one department. There are many budgetary, social and community implications to any development within the institution. The purchase of new furniture for the living unit might delay the hiring of a new teacher, or an improvement in food service might require greater economy in the clothing budget. The administrator's major consideration must be the welfare of the children and the constant improvement of services to them. The totality of the administrator's function sometimes makes him appear aloof or disinterested in the child-care worker's problems.

It is particularly necessary that the child-care worker understands the administrator's function with the community. The administrator has to convince the community of the need for the institution and its progressive development. Sometimes it is desirable to have members of the community visit the institution in order to promote understanding. Such visits may be a burden on the child-care worker. People might walk into the living unit at an inconvenient time. This is regrettable. It is not good for the children to have an undifferentiated stream of visitors coming in. Children and staff should be prepared for such visits. However, the child-care worker must know at all times that he is as much a part of the public relations department as anyone in the institution. His "on the spot" interpretation of the institution's work to strangers might be as important, if not more so, than the interpretation of the administrator himself. The child-care worker must feel that he is not only an employee, but, in a sense, a part of the administration itself.

The Child-Care Worker and the Recreational Worker

Among the specialists working with the children are some recreational workers, such as the coach, the arts and crafts instructor, the librarian, the woodworking instructor, and others. The recreational program depends to a large measure on the interest of the children and the availability of specialists. Quite frequently a child-care worker has enough special skills to lead his own group in these activities and to assume some assignments outside his unit. It is best that the stimulus for special activities comes from within the group and that whatever activity the child engages in outside the unit is based on his activity within it. A child-care worker should not just send children to the arts and crafts shop or the woodwork shop on Monday between 6 P.M. and 8 P.M. He has to participate in the activity, stimulate the child to express himself in recreation, offer ideas as to what he can do, encourage him to pursue his interests and carry them through.

While arts and crafts rooms are valuable, it is even more important for the child to paint a picture in his own living unit when he feels like it. While institutional libraries are desirable, it is even more important that the child can read a book in his own living quarters. The centralization and specialization of recreational activities are most valuable if they are connected with the child's daily life. If a coach finds that a boy tries hard to get accepted on the basketball team, he might ask the child-care worker to practice with this youngster before the team is to be selected. The child-care worker who knows that a child wants to make bookends for his father's birthday should tell the woodwork instructor about this, and perhaps even plan with the child the kind of bookends he can make.

The relationship between the child-care worker and the recreational specialist has to be such that suggestions are easily interchanged. While it might not be feasible nor necessary for them to have regular conferences, some meetings might be needed for the planning of special events.

The Child-Care Worker and the Housekeeping Personnel

We have mentioned how essential food and clothing are to the child. Therefore if the institution has a dietician, it is essential that the child-care worker meet with him to discuss menu planning and review food likes and dislikes. They might have some contacts indirectly through the supervisor, but some of their meetings must be direct. The child-care worker needs to understand the problems of menu planning and the dietician must know the children's attitudes toward food. The same cooperative spirit is needed in contacts with the cooks and maids who work in the unit. Cooks in children's institutions sometimes receive comments only when the food meets with disapproval. All staff members need recognition and support.

The Child-Care Worker and the Maintenance Department

There has to be a good working relationship between the child-care worker and the maintenance workers so that the living unit functions smoothly. The educational and therapeutic planning invested in the institution might be jeopardized by a broken window, a deficient heating system, a leaking water pipe, or a blown fuse. Maintenance workers usually come to the institution not to work with children but to do a good maintenance job. The presence of children may be an inducement or a deterrent. In many institutions, maintenance personnel have played a most helpful role with some children. The child who follows the plumber around in order to "learn" his job gets a feeling of belonging and identification. Some children have their first positive relationship in the institution to the gardener, the truck driver, or the janitor with whom they have a spontaneous rapport.

It cannot, however, be denied that children with disturbances and destructive impulses complicate maintenance workers' jobs. It is important that these staff members understand the agency's attitude toward such behavior.

The child-care worker has to expect that maintenance people will not understand destructiveness and, instead of attributing its causes to the disturbance of the children, may well charge them to the child-care worker's negligence.

Child-care workers in charge of the living unit have to see that it operates as economically and efficiently as possible. One way of achieving this is to prevent deterioration of the building and equipment, by not waiting until things are destroyed or broken down beyond repair. A loose door knob will surely come off or even get lost if it is not fixed immediately. The maintenance work and expenditures are thereby unnecessarily increased. The child-care worker has to regard his unit as though it were his own home and be as efficient and as proud of its physical appearance and upkeep as he would be about his own home. This does not mean that he should regiment the children or put the physical appearance of the unit above their psychological well being. The maintenance worker will respect the child-care worker's work if he feels the child-care worker respects his.

Staff Meetings

Communication is essential to coordinating services. One of the most effective means of communication is the staff meeting. Staff meetings usually have two purposes; one administrative, the other educational. Child-care workers' meetings generally deal with management problems which affect the children's daily living, such as the beginning of school, the preparation of clothing, and medical arrangements. The size and complexity of the institution determine the frequency of these meetings. Occasional meetings of the whole staff are aids to integration. If the subject under discussion warrants it, child-care workers invite others to their meetings.

Child-care workers are usually eager to learn more about their work, to share their experiences with others and to take advantage of learning opportunity offered to them in these staff meetings which help them not only to gain more knowledge in their own field but also to develop greater understanding of the other disciplines. Staff meetings are a necessary part of the job and should be scheduled so that they do not represent an additional burden.

Sometimes professional staff members of the agency can lead these meetings, sometimes outside specialists may have to be called in. In some staff meetings child-care workers themselves can lead the discussion and prepare certain topics in subcommittees. The participation of all child-care workers is needed to utilize all staff meetings as a real learning experience and an aid in the development of teamwork.

All the staff members who work at an institution cannot be mentioned, although some of them play an important part in the life of the children. The psychiatrist and psychologist fulfill in some institutions the functions outlined here for the caseworker (therapist). In others, psychiatrists work as consultants to the caseworkers and have little direct contact with child-care workers. Psychologists in many institutions are specialists in testing the intellectual and emotional capacities of the child, but have little continuous contact with him. The child-care worker has to be aware of their part in the treatment. Cooperation between the medical personnel and the child-care worker is inherent in the program. In some institutions the clergyman plays a vital part in the life of the child. Secretaries, the cashier, business manager, the gardener—in short, everyone—can play an essential role with the child. Everyone is a potential educator and can become an important associate of the child-care worker, and all of them have to be imbued with the spirit of teamwork.

Afterword

The Future of the Child-Care Worker

The child-care worker gives of himself to the utmost in his work. He helps rebuild lives. He gains new insights into human relationships and into himself. Among the staff of the institution he is in the forefront in the campaign to rehabilitate the child. The emotional and intellectual satisfaction that one can get from building up young lives and the value of this work to society cannot ultimately be measured in values of money, status, or education. It has its reward in itself. Nevertheless, satisfactions in terms of social and economic recognition are important. Constant learning is important. Many a child-care worker who did an excellent job for many years has asked himself, "Where do I go from here? How can I use all the knowledge I have gained, the experiences I have accumulated in a broader and more permanent sense, even if I do not want to stay at this particular institution?" Child-care work has yet to be developed into a profession. Many courses have been given, many institutes have been held, many speeches have been made, praising the child-care worker. Yet the security, the status, the advancement and the professional recognition that child-care workers need and deserve have not yet been achieved. Generally recognized professional programs have not been developed. This has to be the next step. A program must be developed which gives child-care workers the possibility of preparing themselves for their profession. The child-care worker will then be able to feel that he is not only filling an important need in a particular institution but that he is a dynamic part of the total field of child-care.

Appendix

**Sample of a Supervisory Conference
between Child-Care Worker and Supervisor**

Miss Janet Brown is twenty-five years old; she has been at the institution for five months and, together with Mrs. Smith and Mr. McDonald, she takes care of a cottage of twelve boys between the ages of nine and eleven. Prior to coming to the institution Miss Brown had worked as an assistant in a nursery school. Before that she had worked in a series of offices as a secretary, managed a store, and had two years of college education.

Mr. White, the supervisor, is a trained group worker whose major function is supervision of child-care workers; he also assists the director in a number of administrative functions. He visits the cottage quite frequently. Before coming to the institution three years ago, Mr. White had worked in a group work agency and prior to graduate school, he had been a counselor in an institution and at a camp. He is twenty-nine years old.

Mr. White sees Miss Brown alone every other week; in the intermittent week he sees her together with Mrs. Smith and Mr. McDonald.

The conference took place at 9:30 in the morning. Miss Brown seemed very tired, sat down and yawned. Mr. White commented that she seemed to be tired and she replied that she had had late duty the evening before and that during the night they had had a number of disturbances. It was her turn to sleep in the cottage. Ronald did not feel well; he vomited a few times and cried; she had to sit with him on his bed for about an hour between one and two in the morning. She had to get up again at 6:30 A.M. and things were very hectic. She had not anticipated the sudden drop in temperature during the night. The children's clothing that had been arranged the night before suddenly had to be changed for winter clothing in the morning. She was on duty together with Mr. McDonald who "knows nothing about clothes." Mrs. Smith had not left the key to one of the lockers and it took some time to go to her room to get them. Mrs. Smith does not like to be disturbed on her day off, but she always forgets to leave the keys. She does not trust anyone else with them. Finally by 8:30 A.M. all the children were out of the cottage and the cottage was in a "big mess." The kids had been very much upset about the sudden change in clothing. She commented that she was glad she was in Mr. White's office where she could at least sit calmly and smoke a cigaret.

Mr. White commented that there were three or four major areas of trouble: first, Ronnie's sickness at night; second, the long hours and the continuation from late shift to morning shift; third, Mr. McDonald's inability to handle clothing; and fourth, Mrs. Smith's monopolizing the keys. Miss Brown added that of course there was another problem, but she could not hold the institution responsible for that—the change in weather. They both laughed; then Mr. White said that apparently she holds the institution responsible for all her other problems. Miss Brown was a little embarrassed and indicated she did not mean it this way. However, the work is harder than she had anticipated; some of the problems could be eliminated "if only people would want to cooperate." She likes Mr. McDonald a lot. He is kind to the children and they have a lot of fun with each other. However, he does not know a thing about housekeeping, clothing, or setting the table. He is very young and is "just a man—almost a boy himself." "At least he admits it when he doesn't know something," she added. This morning he came to her and said he did not know what the children should wear because of the sudden cold wave. Miss Brown would have to take the initiative.

The supervisor asked if she were angry with Mr. McDonald for that. She said no, on the contrary, she felt that it was an honest statement—only it made more work for her. She had the same situation at home when she was living with her parents. After her mother died her older brother and father came to her for everything. She made all the decisions. Mr. White commented that it was good there was a woman around this morning. If Mr. McDonald had happened to be on duty alone—which had occurred a few times before—he probably would not have known what to do. Miss Brown laughed and said he probably would not even have noticed that there was a cold wave. But she is glad there is a man around, especially in the afternoon, when the children come home. He takes them out for swimming and for all kinds of activities that she cannot do so well.

It seems that everybody in the cottage should know where everything is, exactly, and there should be a rule as to who has the keys. Mr. White indicated that there is such a rule: that the person on duty must have the keys. Apparently Mrs. Smith forgot about the rule. Miss Brown said that Mrs. Smith forgets too often about these things; actually she does not want to give the keys to anybody else. She wants to run the cottage all by herself, and in a way she resents Miss Brown's presence as well as Mr. McDonald's.

Mr. White wondered why. Miss Brown said that she thought that Mrs. Smith, who had been in the institution for eleven years, still remembered the time when there had been only one cottage mother to a unit and when the whole system of child-care workers was not yet established. Now they have two people on duty all the time, "which is absolutely necessary," but Mrs. Smith fears that part of her authority is being taken from her. Mr. White wondered whether it might be hard for Mrs. Smith to share the administrative duties of the cottage with the others; she had done the job pretty well alone for a long time and maybe she could not understand why there had to be more people. Miss Brown added that Mrs. Smith herself said that she could not do it alone but then she said: "Well, I guess it must be hard if somebody comes into your home and says, 'Now I'm sharing this home with you.'" Maybe it was a wise idea for Mrs. Smith to have the keys all by herself, except when she is off duty.

Usually she arranges everything ahead of time. She arranges all the clothing for the children before going off duty. She had done it this time, too, but she had not figured on the cold wave. Miss Brown added that usually Mrs. Smith is very cooperative. For instance, last week Miss Brown's brother was in town and Mrs. Smith offered to change her day off so that Miss Brown could be free while her brother was around. Miss Brown was very grateful for this offer. Actually, she added, that was why her late duty yesterday fell together with her early duty today. Mr. White laughed and said it was really because of Mrs. Smith's changing with her that she got into all this trouble these last two days. If Mrs. Smith had not changed with her, she would have been off today. Miss Brown said it was really funny that Mrs. Smith's cooperativeness led to calling her uncooperative. Mr. White indicated that it was nevertheless probably correct that Mrs. Smith had a lot of feeling that new workers coming in had the same amount of authority that she had after ten years of service, and maybe the others had to understand that in order to work with her. At the next meeting of the group, he will discuss this whole problem of keys again.

Mr. White recognized that Mrs. Smith and Mr. McDonald had their good and their bad features, and that sometimes it was not easy to work with them. Miss Brown said that she herself had problems. Mr. White asked what she meant. She said she becomes easily discouraged; sometimes she loses her temper with the children too readily. Mrs. Smith never loses her temper. She is always calm with them. Miss Brown went on. She had lost her temper during the night with Ronnie. Mr. White asked her to tell him about Ronnie. She told him of knowing that Ronnie had bad dreams at night, sometimes waking up and vomiting. The caseworker had told her that this had something to do with the fact that Ronnie's parents were getting a divorce at this time, and that the boy was worried about it. Ronnie never talked about this problem with the caseworker or with any other staff member; however, at night he is restless, does not sleep, and in the middle of the night he wakes up with stomach-aches. The caseworker said it was necessary just to sit up with him for a while and to be kind to him. She had tried to do that. She had sat up with him many a night during the past few weeks.

However, last night, after he had vomited and felt better again, he wanted her to sit next to him on his bed. He did not say anything but just wanted her to be there, and each time she started to go back to her bed he started crying. While she was sitting with him, however, he talked very loud. He was hungry and wanted a glass of milk. She did not think he should have milk just after he had vomited, so she told him she could not get it for him now. Ronnie then said he would wake up all the other children, whereupon she became very angry. She actually felt like giving him a spanking. She took him into a room where there were no other children. This was pretty rough on him, she thought. However, she was exhausted and angry and while in the other room she told him that now he had to be quiet. She was very tired and wanted some sleep. He fell asleep soon thereafter and then she went back to her bed.

Mr. White asked what she regretted most. She said, two things: one was that she had told him he was a faker, that he was completely well and just wanted to keep her up. She would not say that if she were not angry, because she does not really believe he was faking. She just felt that he was feeling somewhat better and wanted her to stay up with him. Mr. White asked if he came up to her during the daytime too. Miss Brown said yes, he does it very often. He runs up to her, hangs around her, wants to be near her. Mr. White asked if she was glad that he seeks her out. She said yes. Some children seem to cling more to Mrs. Smith, but he seems to cling more to her. She does not know why. Once he asked if he could call her "Mommy." She told him then that he had his own mommy and he said to her, well, he wants to have another mommy for safety. Mr. White talked with Miss Brown about this boy's fear of losing his mother and at the same time his anxiety about deserting her.

While Mr. White thought it was right that she told Ronnie she was not his mommy, he felt it was good that she showed the child she was really interested in him. Mr. White did not think it so bad if at times one got angry at a child, as long as one showed the child in many other ways that one really liked him. She had been with him a good part of the night, which undid any harm that her scolding might have done.

Mr. White asked her what the second thing was that she regretted. She regretted that she had told Ronnie: "I wish that your caseworker would sit next to you sometimes and see your behavior." Why did she say this? Miss Brown explained that the caseworkers somehow expect the child-care workers to do things that they themselves would never do. For instance, would a caseworker get up in the middle of the night for three weeks in a row for a child? Yet the caseworker will tell the child-care worker to do just that. Mr. White pointed out that the caseworkers really had no right to tell them what to do. They could only explain to them what the children's problems were or what would be best for the children. No caseworker has the right to tell her that she has to get up at night. Miss Brown said that the caseworker did not really do that. Actually, she liked and admired the caseworkers very much, she said, and looked forward to her talks with them. The caseworker had told her that the boy was very upset these days and was afraid and confused about the divorce. When the boy became restless and started vomiting, she, on her own, wanted to give him some special attention and began staying up with him at night. She had not wanted him to feel that he was going to lose her at the same time that he was afraid of losing his home. Mr. White pointed out that it really was not the caseworker who was the cause of her sitting up with the boy at night. Miss Brown said no, it was she herself. "But," she added, "they tell you so many things about the children that you feel very guilty if you don't try to do what they think is best."

Mr. White felt that she tried maybe a little too hard. "If a child needs an adult every night, we must either have a night supervisor for him or send him to the infirmary. We do not expect any child-care worker to work day and night. As a matter of fact, in this institution we are not equipped to help a child who needs attention every night. Only the infirmary has day and night service." Miss Brown was very much against Ronnie's being sent there. This was bad for the child, she said, she would rather get twice as tired as she now is than see that happen. She thought that in a few weeks Ronnie would be all right again.

Mr. White thought it would be possible to shift the working time so that for the time being somebody would be available until later at night and would not have to get up so early in the morning. Miss Brown thought this would be a satisfactory temporary solution. Usually Ronnie's night terrors occur around 12:30 A.M. Therefore, if somebody were on duty at that time for a few weeks (the official day-time duty is over at ten o'clock, then one of the child-care workers sleeps in) and could stay up until one and maybe start correspondingly later the next day, this could be arranged. She really did not want to have the child out of the unit. Mr. White indicated that she really had a lot of feeling for this child. She said she liked him. He is a nice but very unhappy child and she thinks "we can help him. We should stand by him now." Mr. White pointed out that this feeling she had for the child was very helpful and probably more important than anything else, even though she sometimes got angry with him. She smiled and said she is not angry with him any more at all.

Mr. White arranged for meetings with Mrs. Smith and Mr. McDonald this same day about the new schedule. He said that he might be able to hire a part-time student counselor to help out for a few hours in the afternoon.

Mr. White wondered if there was anything else new in the cottage. Miss Brown did not think there was. He wondered how the birthday party for Charles had worked out. (The party was about six days before the conference.) Miss Brown said she was glad he reminded her of that because she forgot to mention to him that she thinks Mr. McDonald should always be in on birthday parties because he knows so many games. She herself has learned to play many games since she has been in the group, but it is better if Mr. McDonald leads the games. He has a way of introducing games which she really admires. Mr. McDonald usually introduces a new game at each birthday; then the children play it for a long time and look forward to the next birthday to learn a new one. This time Mr. McDonald was not around for the birthday party; there was no new game and the children were disappointed. They ate their cake and ice cream but something was missing.

Mr. White wondered why she could not learn some of the methods of Mr. McDonald. She said it was hard for her, but she might try. Mr. White wondered if possibly each of the three counselors could learn from the other. Mr. McDonald might learn from her and Mrs. Smith something about the children's clothing and all the linens in the cottage, while they might learn from him a little bit about games. Miss Brown said that the children do not expect Mrs. Smith to play games with them; they just expect her to be around and organize things, but from herself they expect games. She wondered if there were books on games, and Mr. White indicated there were some in the institution's library but he could recommend others which could be found at the public library. He could also have Mr. McDonald talk a little bit about the way he plays games at one of their joint conferences. He was sure Miss Brown would soon be able to do a good job at leading games, even though she might do it differently from Mr. McDonald.

There was nothing else, she indicated, but upon Mr. White's reminder, she remembered there was some other trouble. She had made requisitions three or four times already for repairs of the bathroom pipes, which were stopped up, but everything works so slowly. The maintenance supervisor had told her that a piece of pipe had to be replaced; it would take another week before they could get it. The children had put some cement-like chemical into one of the pipes. The maintenance man was furious at the children and the staff of the cottage. Now they can only use three instead of five basins and there is a terrible rush every morning and evening. Mr. White commented that the maintenance man had complained about them and that he, too, was concerned about this, because apparently there had not been sufficient supervision of the washing of the children who had put the chemical into the sink unobserved.

Miss Brown indicated that Paul and Richard had done this. Those two boys had been in trouble all the time. One day they had to have matches taken away from them, the next day they played with the electricity, and then they got involved in this kind of thing. It is impossible to supervise them all that intensely. Mr. White wondered if they knew that the children possessed this chemical. She said they did not know but might have suspected something. The two children had acted peculiarly around their lockers. She looked through Paul's and Dick's belongings to find out whether they had any further equipment that might be used destructively. Dick and Paul have been punished; in the future they can play only when an adult is around. They also have to remove the locks from their lockers. But the bathroom must be fixed.

Mr. White sympathized with her on the trouble she had. He wondered whether the job was worth all the anguish. Miss Brown said it was very hard but still she loves it. Slowly she feels that she understands the children and that most of them like her. It was very hard in the beginning when she did not know anything about the children. Right now she feels that the children are "also mine and that I have something to say about them and maybe can help them a little bit." In the beginning she felt somehow they were only Mrs. Smith's children and the caseworkers'. She said that she felt much better now after having talked things over, and she hoped that the matters of the late hours and leaving the keys when off duty could be arranged. Mr. White assured her that these things would be settled.

As she was ready to leave, Mr. White told her that the following week he wanted to meet with her, Mrs. Smith, and Mr. McDonald, to discuss the spending of cottage funds, and also he would like to make some plans for the forthcoming vacation period of the children. The following week, he suggested, since she had been here for almost half a year now, they would discuss her evaluation, and she was asked to think over in the meantime what she thought of her work, in which areas she considered herself successful, and in which she felt she had failed.

COMMENT

In this supervisory conference the child-care worker came in with a number of problems and a good deal of anger about certain difficulties in the unit and about her own acts. The supervisor helped her to clarify some of these things, to see what the major problems were and organize them in a way so that she saw the three or four major problems she was confronted with. Seeing these as clearly circumscribed, individual problems and not one big problem made it a lot easier for her to look at them and to tackle them. The relationship between her and the supervisor was one of confidence and forthrightness. Miss Brown brought to the supervisor her feelings of jealousy of Mrs. Smith, her ambivalence about caseworkers, her anger at Ronnie, her dissatisfaction with the maintenance, and her questions about the administration, but she could also discuss her own mistakes. Mr. White did not minimize or deny these problems but he encouraged her to see also the positive elements within herself and her co-workers. He suggested some methods whereby some of the concrete problems could be solved. At the end of the conference Miss Brown obviously felt better, saw things more clearly and was less overwhelmed by them than at the beginning.

Index

Group recreational activity (*cont.*)
participation, 127, 128; duration of,
128; spontaneity, 125; *see also* Recreational activity
Group-rejected child, The, 51–54

Handicaps: and institutional placement,
5
Health, 85–88; sleep requirements, 116
Homemaking, 101–105
Homework, 109–110, 165
Homosexual excitement: control of, 82–
83
Housekeeping personnel, 168

Illness, 86–88; psychological meaning
of, 86–88
Infirmary: use of, 86–87
In-group, The, 28, 29–37
Institutional placement: history of, 4;
prevention of, 5; purpose of, 5, 11,
16; reasons for, 3–6, 11
Inter-staff communication, 14, 153; evaluation conferences, 160–161; staff
meetings, 170–171
Inter-staff relationships: cooperation,
155–157; frictions, 156
Isolates, 28–29, 46–55

Letter writing, 110–111

Mail, 106–107
Maintenance department, 169, 170
Meals, 57–75; atmosphere, 71–72; beginning and ending, 74; breakfast, 70–
71; duration of, 74–75; packed
lunches, 71–72; serving, 72–73; table
conversation, 75; table manners, 73–
74
Meetings: evaluation, 160–161; staff, 170–
171
Menstruation: giving information about,
85
Menu planning, 68–69

Needs of child: *see* Child, needs of
New child, The, 46–48
New child-care worker, The, 151
Night attendants, 117

Parents: attitudes toward institutional
placement, 4; importance to children, 144–145
Parent-child relationship: information
on, 147

Personal hygiene, 82–85
Personality traits: origin of, 7–8
Petty cash fund, 112
Privacy, 23–24, 43
Punishment, 140–143; incorrect forms
of, 141–142; logical application of,
140–141; psychological fitness of,
141; timing of, 142

Records, 11–15, 160
Recreational activity, 118–133; ability to
accept rules, 123–124; ability to lose,
124; and the outside community,
132; as ego builder, 119; competitive elements, 124, 129–131; emotional implications, 120, 121, 122; enjoyment of, 118–119; group, 125–128;
social value of, 121, 123; solitary,
120–123; television, 131–132; voluntary nature of, 119; with others,
123–125
Recreational worker, The, 167–168
Religious education, 115
Routines, 77–117; activities, individual
and scheduled, 107–109; after
school, 105–106; bedtime, 115–117;
chores, 95–99; dressing, 88–89; function of, 78–79; homemaking, 101–
105; personal hygiene, 82–85; the
rising hour, 80–81; school preparations, 99–101

Scheduling: *see* Routines
School, 99–101, 165; vocational training,
113
Separation: effects of, 7
Sexual development: observation of, 85
Sleep: necessary amount of, 116
Snacks, 75–76, 106
Staff communication, 14, 153, 170–171
Staff meetings, 170–171
Sub-groups: *see* Cliques and sub-groups
Supervision: purposes of, 157–158
Supervisory relationship, 159–161

Table manners, 73–74
Teacher, 164–166
Teamwork, 150–171; neighborliness, 153;
respect for contribution of others,
151–153

Vocational training, 113

Withdrawn child, The, 49–50
Work programs, 113–114